The Temperament God Gave Your Spouse

by
Art Bennett, LMFT
and
Laraine Bennett

SOPHIA INSTITUTE PRESS®
Manchester, New Hampshire

Sophia Institute Press®
Box 5284, Manchester, NH 03108
1-800-888-9344
www.sophiainstitute.com

Library of Congress Cataloging-in-Publication Data

Bennett, Art.
    The temperament God gave your spouse / by Art and Laraine Bennett.
        p. cm.
    ISBN 978-1-933184-30-2 (pbk. : alk. paper)
    1. Marriage — Religious aspects — Christianity. 2. Temperament — Religious aspects — Christianity. I. Bennett, Laraine. II. Title.
    BV835.B443 2008
    248.8'44 — dc22

                                                            2008019526

09 10 11 12 13 9 8 7 6 5 4 3 2

To Pope Benedict XVI

∞

Contents

∞

Acknowledgments

We are deeply grateful to William and Teje Etchemendy for their beautiful example of a long, happy marriage spanning six decades. We are also grateful to Art and Mildred Bennett and Art's brothers and sisters for their prayerful support and love. We also wish to thank all our friends and colleagues who shared with us their temperament stories — especially our children, who provided much material (we hope they forgive us!).

We are also grateful to our friend and pastor, Father Francis Peffley; and to our spiritual director, Father John Hopkins, L.C., a man whose unbounded zeal for souls inspires us, and whose spiritual guidance is always Christ-centered and insightful. We are grateful for the professional insights of Dr. Frank Moncher, Dr. William Nordling, and Chris and Mary Anne Yep. We also want to thank everyone at the Alpha Omega Clinics and Triune Health Group for their insights, support, and professionalism.

Finally, we thank our editor, Todd Aglialoro, who at last admitted to his true temperament, and whose vision and masterful editing brings out the best in us, and makes the final product a harmonious whole.

∽

Preface

Someone once remarked that marriage has three rings: the engagement ring, the wedding ring, and suffering! The saying has a vein of truth, and it refers not so much to the occasional traumatic events all married couples experience through life, but more to the everyday trials, annoyances, and irritations that arise due to the couple's contrasting (and often conflicting) personality types.

Over the course of eighteen years as a Catholic priest, I've had the opportunity and privilege of preparing over five hundred engaged couples for marriage. During the Pre-Cana meetings, I've always introduced them to the four-temperaments concept and had each couple take the simple test to determine who they are "temperamentally."

Three years ago, when Art and Laraine Bennett published their first book, *The Temperament God Gave You*, I was delighted to be able to give each couple a copy to read and study. The results were marvelous! So many of the couples have since told me how much they learned from it, about themselves and about each other, and how much better prepared they felt to be future partners in marriage.

Now Art and Laraine have given me another tool for my pastorate: this specialized book for married couples who haven't fully experienced the benefits of understanding the temperaments. It shows how knowledge of the temperaments can enrich a marriage by opening the way to deeper intimacy, more-effective communication, and greater and interpersonal compatibility. It will be especially helpful to me and my fellow priests as we are called upon to counsel couples who are experiencing difficulties in their marriage — many of which are caused by an unawareness of the effects of temperament on personality.

The Bennetts are to be congratulated for giving us this tested, beneficial, and grace-filled approach to marital happiness, personal growth, and, ultimately, the strengthening of the Church and society.

Rev. Francis J. Peffley, Pastor
Holy Trinity Church
Gainesville, VA

∞

The Temperament
God Gave Your Spouse

Part 1

∞

The Temperaments and Marriage

Chapter 1

∽

What Is Temperament?

"Conjugal love involves a totality,
in which all the elements of the person enter."
Catechism of the Catholic Church, no. 1643

"Between you two there must come sometime
Peace . . . though you be not of one temperament."
Geoffrey Chaucer

∞

Stacy is a vivacious and energetic mom who volunteers at her children's school and for her parish, shuttles her five kids to their many extracurricular activities, and even runs her own home-based sales business. Her husband, Ron, is a quiet and thoughtful medical researcher who relishes time alone, reading or playing the piano.

When Stacy and Ron first married, they enjoyed their widely differing personalities. Stacy admired Ron's sensitivity and his depth of reflection, his meticulous attention to detail, and his sense of order and purpose. Ron chuckled indulgently over Stacy's fun, impromptu adventures and was intrigued by her larger social circle.

But once the kids began to come and the pressures of work and family increased, Ron found himself drained by all the hustle and bustle of Stacy's life. He needed time to "decompress" after work, but Stacy wanted to talk about her day or rush off to a meeting as soon as Ron walked in the door. Stacy began to complain of suffering from an "emotional vacuum" because Ron rarely wanted to talk. When she badgered him, Ron only withdrew further into unwelcoming silence.

Ron and Stacy reacted to each other this way because they have completely opposite *temperaments*: Ron is a deeply sensitive *melancholic* who requires time for silence and reflection, while Stacy is a lively, talkative *sanguine* who needs abundant interpersonal interaction. And it was not until Ron and Stacy were able to understand — and accept — each other's temperaments that they were able to avoid misunderstandings and hurt feelings, and to make their marriage the strong, loving union it had once been.[1]

Grace builds on nature and nurture

The human personality is mysterious and complex. Psychologists have long debated exactly how heredity (the genetic traits we're born with) and our environment (our parents, education, culture, and so on) combine to impact the development of our personality. Regardless of the precise manner in which this happens, we can safely assert that the human personality is a dynamic amalgam of both "nature" and "nurture." Furthermore, our Christian faith tells us that the human person, created in the image and likeness of God, is never *determined* by his environment or his genes, but is fundamentally *free*. Our human personality, then, is influenced by biological and environmental factors, but is also critically impacted by our own free will — the way we respond to our environment, to our nature, and to God's grace.

It is in these responses, in our patterns of reaction, that we locate our *temperament*.

In our first book, *The Temperament God Gave You*, we re-introduced the concept of the "classic" four temperaments: choleric, melancholic, sanguine, and phlegmatic. We showed how understanding our own temperament helps us grow in self-knowledge, improve our relationships with our friends and family, motivate our children, and even deepen our spiritual life. In this book we're going to look in much greater detail at how understanding our

---

[1] Ron and Stacy first appeared in our article "Know Yourself, Know Your Spouse," in the June 2007 issue of *The Word Among Us*.

temperament — and our spouse's — can lead us to happier, richer, and holier marriages.

Preloaded at the factory

The concept of the classic four temperaments dates back 2,000 years to Hippocrates, the "father of medical science." He held that differences in personalities were caused by an individual's predominant bodily fluid — hence, the rather unappealing names! The "sanguine" temperament was thought to be eager and optimistic; the "melancholic" reticent and somewhat doleful; the "choleric" passionate; and the "phlegmatic" calm.

The scientific rationale for the temperaments was bad (we no longer think about personality in terms of bodily fluids!), but the concept of the four temperaments was good, and it's just as useful for us today as it was in Hippocrates's time.

We are each born with one of the four as our primary temperament, indicating our natural predisposition to react in certain ways — our "default setting," so to speak. God has given each of us a tendency or inclination to react quickly or slowly, intensely or calmly, and to hold only to that reaction for a long or a short period. This tendency affects the rest of our personality: our emotionality, sociability, attention, and prevailing moods.

How quickly do we react to a person or an idea? How strongly do we react when we are praised or chastised, or when we are pressed for an opinion? Are we short-tempered, or easygoing? Do we tend to look on the bright side, or do we take a more pessimistic approach? Do we tend to mull things over for a long time before we respond, or do we fire off an opinion from the top of our heads? Are we easily distractible or intensely focused?

Because such reactions are both part of our inborn nature and reinforced by lifelong habit, we may not even realize that we are thinking, acting, or reacting in any particular way at all, much less in a way indicative of a temperament. So a little self-reflection might be in order.

Ask yourself:

❑ Do I respond quickly or slowly when presented with an idea, a situation, or a person?

❑ Do I react intensely or not intensely?

❑ Do I hold on to that reaction for a long time or a short time?

❑ Am I focused internally (inner world of thoughts and feelings) or externally (action in the world)?

❑ Do I tend to think relationally or logically? Do I make decisions based on feelings or principles?

❑ Am I energized by (or tend to dwell in) the external, social world? Or am I more highly attuned to my internal world of thoughts and feelings?

The four temperaments in a nutshell

The *choleric* is your original "type A" personality: he wants to take charge and get things done. If that leads to conflict, so much the better! (Choleric president Franklin Delano Roosevelt put it well: "There is nothing I love so much as a good fight.") Cholerics exhibit quick, intense, sustained reactions to both external and internal stimuli. Cholerics are decisive, determined, and goal-oriented. They are dynamic, self-motivated, forceful, and confident.

But in dealing with others, they are sometimes accused of rolling over people once they have set a plan in motion, of being stubborn and demanding, opinionated, argumentative, and irascible.

Cholerics make great saints . . . or great sinners. St. Paul was a driven and brilliant Pharisee who laid waste to the early Christian community; after his conversion he was equally zealous in spreading the gospel.

"What a great guy!" is a typical epithet for the easygoing *phlegmatic*. The key to the phlegmatic is that he is a peacemaker: he hates conflict, especially interpersonal conflict. Thus, the phlegmatic is the polar opposite of the choleric. Where the choleric is a driven leader, the phlegmatic is docile and cooperative. Where the choleric relishes a good argument, the phlegmatic just wants everyone to get along. Phlegmatics are dependable, polite, and eventempered. Phlegmatics tend to feel more comfortable in a small group of friends or even spending a quiet evening relaxing at home. They would rather take the blame (even unjustly) than stir up controversy. They tend to be of few words, and favor a quiet, dry wit.

In relationships, phlegmatics are steady and stabilizing, reliable and willing to make concessions. Under stress, however, they tend to withdraw; because they do not react quickly and are not very talkative, you can be tempted to nag them. St. Thomas Aquinas is thought to have been a brilliant phlegmatic. As G. K. Chesterton wrote, "His curiously simple character, his lucid but laborious intellect, could not be better summed up than by saying he did not know how to sneer."[2] It is said of St. Thomas that his last confession was so pure and simple, it could have been the confession of a five-year-old child.

Who doesn't love a *sanguine*? The sanguine is your classic "people person" — the life of the party, fun-loving, and talkative. Sanguines have quick, intense, but short-lived reactions. They live in

[2] G. K. Chesterton, *St. Thomas Aquinas: The Dumb Ox* (New York: Doubleday, 1956).

the present moment, and prefer that moment to be full of company and activity. The sanguine temperament is interested, optimistic, and enthusiastic — but forgetful. They tend to be the ones who impulsively volunteer for many things and wind up overcommitted.

Sanguines want to be loved (that's *why* they're standing on the table wearing the lampshade!). They want to be happy — and they want *you* to be happy *with them*. As a result, in relationships they are affectionate and generous, and opt for doing plenty of fun things together, but they can be rather skittish about facing anything negative. St. Peter was a loveable-but-inconstant sanguine. "Lord, I am prepared to go to prison and to die with you," he fervently pronounces; a few hours later, Peter denies even knowing Jesus![3] When Christ appears walking on the water, Peter impulsively joins him — until he begins to sink.[4]

It is said that the melancholic so longs for heaven that everything on earth falls short. Melancholics are known for their deep introspection, the depth and vehemence of their sentiments, and their nobility of purpose. Critical perfectionists, melancholics are cautious, somewhat pessimistic, detail-oriented, and serious.

Melancholics are choosy about their friends, but unwaveringly loyal and persevering. They have long memories both of kindness and of slights. Melancholics are accordingly drawn to the spiritual life and to noble causes; counselors, parish priests, humanitarians, and artists are often melancholics. It is suggested that St. John the Evangelist was a melancholic. The beloved disciple was the only one of the apostles who remained at the Crucifixion, and the one to whom Jesus entrusted his mother. Of all the four Gospels, St. John's is the most poetic and profound.

[3] Luke 22:56-60.
[4] Cf. Matt. 14:30.

What Is Temperament?

Why can't everyone be like me?

Just as we are often unaware of our own pattern of reactions, we often fail to appreciate how people with different temperaments can have widely differing reactions to the same stimuli. For example, one night the two of us were seated at a dinner table at a fundraiser for our son's football team. Decorating the table were photographs and articles about the team, fixed upside down under a clear plastic tablecloth. Choleric Laraine immediately pulled up the cloth and peeled off the photographs, to be able to see them better.

"That's the difference between you and me," phlegmatic Art said. "I wanted to read the articles, too, but I didn't think I ought to rearrange the table decorations. I resigned myself to looking at them upside down."

The ability to appreciate other people's temperaments is especially important in marriage, because opposite temperaments tend to attract each other, as with Ron and Stacy. It is often the case that we will *like* people who have temperaments similar to ours, but we will *fall in love* with those of opposite temperaments. The strengths and weaknesses of each are attractively complementary: the sociable and easily distracted sanguine finds seriousness and depth in the orderly melancholic — who, in turn, is drawn out of himself by the sanguine's lightness of heart. The peaceful phlegmatic seems made for a strong-willed, take-charge choleric, who both challenges and learns patience from his more docile mate. But what initially attracts can also soon become a source of irritation.

Stella Chess and Alexander Thomas, pioneers in the study of temperament, warn that "a marital problem can develop and escalate if one or both partners . . . assume that such a behavioral pattern is somehow a matter of choice and represents a *willful refusal* to make a change 'for the better.' " In such a case, they explain, "the inconvenience or frustration that the one partner's temperament creates for the other is interpreted as another evidence of willful intent to annoy and harass."[5] Understanding temperament helps diffuse such misunderstandings by creating an atmosphere of *respect* — for the wonderful way God made me and my spouse — and by restoring positive communication in place of resentment, nagging, and false accusations.

Stacy and Ron had become caught in just such a downward spiral, each charging that the other was *intentionally* reacting in ways designed to irritate and leave their emotional needs unmet. But when they were led to discover how deeply rooted their reactions were in their nature, in their God-given temperament (which, as such, is inherently *good*), they grew in *acceptance* and *empathy*. They realized they could make minor concessions that would honor each other's temperament and meet each other's needs.

Instead of thinking that Stacy was a scatterbrained chatterbox, Ron began to understand her deep need for abundant and expressive communication. Stacy began to accept Ron's periods of silence as vitally necessary to recharge his batteries — rather than assuming he was being "antisocial." Stacy learned how to wait until Ron had fulfilled his need for quiet time, and strategically chose times when he felt most refreshed — say, early on a Saturday morning, over coffee — to bring up serious issues to talk about. When Ron's need for introspective time and space had been met, he had more energy and was able to join Stacy in some of her more social ventures, instead of moodily complaining all the time.

[5] Stella Chess, M.D., and Alexander Thomas, M.D., *Temperament in Clinical Practice* (New York: The Guilford Press, 1986), 108 ff; our emphasis.

Love . . . and temperament

Temperament affects not only our deepest emotional needs, but also our moods, the way we think and communicate, and even the way we pray. Since marriage is a sacrament, designed to lead spouses to heaven, temperament's influence on prayer and the spiritual life can't be ignored.

In fact, throughout the history of the Church, the concept of temperament has been used as a means to aid spiritual development through growth in self-knowledge. Self-knowledge requires understanding the *whole person* — our emotions and passions, natural tendencies and reactions — as well as our virtues and spiritual gifts. Many of the great saints, such as Thomas Aquinas and Francis de Sales, as well as respected theologians such as the Reverend Adolphe Tanquerey and Father Jordan Aumann, O.P., and Pope John Paul I, have written about temperament and how it helps us in our human and spiritual formation. Understanding temperament helps us grow in empathy, in understanding, and in delicate charity — enabling us to show our loved ones how deeply we care about them, so that we can become that "intimate community of life and love" that we are meant to be.[6]

∞

As we explore the different kinds of temperaments and how they interact in the marital relationship, keep in mind that our descriptions represent the temperament in its pure or idealized form, and that most people are not purely one temperament, but are rather a combination or blend of temperaments, yet always with one temperament that is primary. In our first book, *The Temperament God Gave You*, we examined blended temperaments in some

[6] *Catechism of the Catholic Church* (CCC), no. 1603.

detail, and we recommend that you read those sections to gain a fuller picture of your unique temperament blend.

In this book we won't be revisiting temperament types and blends nearly as thoroughly; we *will* be looking at how temperament impacts your vocation as a spouse, exploring the complex and wonderful interplay between different temperaments within marriage.

∞

"The Lord God said: 'It is not good for man to be alone. I will make a suitable partner for him' . . ."

Read Genesis 2:18-24. Then, as you read this book, ask yourself:

❑ What is a "suitable partner"?

❑ Is it about always agreeing with me? Doing what I say?

❑ Do I need to control my spouse or always have the final say?

❑ Do I expect my spouse to answer all my emotional needs?

❑ Did I marry my partner to "fix him [or her]"?

❑ How do I need to change the way I view our marriage, so that it more closely resembles what God intends for it?

Chapter 2

∞

The Four Kinds of Spouses

∽

Quiz: What Kind of Spouse Are You?

1. Your spouse is driving you and the kids to the grocery store. You notice that the gas gauge indicates you are getting close to empty.

❏ You gasp, "We'll never make it to the store! I told you to get gas the last time we were out. Pull over at the nearest gas station!" Then you begin to say Hail Marys.

❏ You shrug, "Oh, we'll probably make it. There is always some left even when it's on empty."

❏ You don't say anything, because you never looked at the gas gauge.

❏ You are driving. Your spouse is in the passenger seat.

2. Your spouse surprises you by coming home for lunch and saying he has the rest of the day free — to spend with you!

❏ You are rather annoyed, because you had already planned your day.

❏ You say, "I'll just cancel everything else, and let's go shopping, out to lunch, and maybe we can even catch a movie without the kids . . ."

❏ You are a bit embarrassed because you still haven't gotten the morning dishes put away, because after you dropped the kids off at school, you stayed a long time just chatting with the office secretary.

❑ You aren't home because you are at your monthly board meeting.

3. The kitchen sink is completely backed up, and when you call the plumber, you discover that he is out of town for the weekend.

❑ You flip out. You simply cannot go a day without the use of a garbage disposal. You tell your spouse that he needs to get a plumber *immediately* or somehow fix it.

❑ You call your neighbor and ask for a recommendation on a plumber, and then chat for a half-hour about the neighborhood, the kids, the weather, and the state of the housing market.

❑ You say, "Oh, well, we can use the bathroom sink for a few days until our plumber gets back in town."

❑ You fix it yourself, even if you have never had any plumbing experience. Then you gloat about how you fixed it all by yourself.

In this (admittedly exaggerated for humor's sake) quiz, the first answer to each question points to a melancholic, the second to a sanguine, the third a phlegmatic and the last a choleric. As spouses, each will have temperamentally characteristic ways of approaching the fundamental aspects of marriage, such as work, parenting, and intimacy. In this chapter we'll look at those characteristics more closely. See if you can recognize yourself, and your spouse!

YOUR COMMANDING CHOLERIC COMPANION

"It was going to be one of Rabbit's busy days. As soon as he woke up he felt important, as if everything depended upon him. It was just the day for Organizing Something . . . a Captainish sort of day, when everybody said, 'Yes, Rabbit' and 'No, Rabbit,' and waited until he had told them."

A. A. Milne, *The World of Pooh*

Your choleric spouse is a natural leader, motivator, and initiator. He is ambitious, a quick learner, and adept at many things. He loves to take charge and wants everyone to respect the fact that he is *right* — if not always, then ninety-nine percent of the time. He is extraverted, productive, dynamic, and confrontational. He values loyalty (to himself and to his family) at all costs. Whether in a man or woman, this temperament is competitive, decisive, pragmatic, and always on the go. (Don't bother trying to get your choleric husband to read this book. You'll have to catch him on the fly — reading snippets to him as he takes a shower or leaving messages on his voicemail.)

Your choleric spouse aims to be a successful provider, whether he is the primary breadwinner or a secondary contributor. He puts his abundant energy to work in many arenas: in the workforce or a home business, volunteering for church or school, and running the family. You will rarely catch him lazing around the house, watching TV, or wasting time. Even running routine errands will be conducted with an eye to efficiency. Choleric Frank Gilbreth (an industrial engineer whose family life was recorded by his children in *Cheaper by the Dozen*) required his family to "count motions" to make sure they did every task — even shaving, showering, and getting dressed — with as few wasted moments as possible!

The choleric may even be so efficient a worker and manager, that other, less "productive" (in his view) aspects of his life suffer. You may have to keep an eye out to make sure your choleric spouse makes time for "unproductive" but necessary pursuits such as prayer, relaxation, and just spending time with his family — *not* coaching you to be more efficient, *not* pushing your kids to excel in a sport, but simply being together. For choleric Laraine, playing Candyland with small children was sheer torture. During games of hide-and-seek, she was sorely tempted to hide in a closet and work on a writing project.

The choleric in love

Since the choleric tends to throw himself into achieving his goals, he can be an energetic suitor. The choleric in love may be suave, fascinating, talkative, persuasive, attentive, affectionate — whatever it takes — to win his heart's desire. He may also express impatience to keep the relationship moving forward toward the high expectations he has set for it. Once married, though, a choleric's priorities may shift — since he will have achieved his goal — and he'll turn the same energy toward earning a living, raising a family, and keeping up a house. In such cases, the spouse of a choleric may wonder, "What happened to that romantic creature?"

The truth is, cholerics are not really romantic by nature. They are impulsive and loyal; they can be charming and debonair; but the slower pace and lingering affect of true romance can be quite foreign to them. A male choleric, especially, can be puzzled by the ordeals of candlelight dinners and intimate conversation, and just want to get to the business at hand. He may likewise be willing to forgo intimacy in favor of sex.

Cholerics struggle with the emotional realm: because they are so goal-oriented, so capable of fixing their minds and wills on a goal, tuning out all distractions and ignoring their own *feelings* in order to attain it, they tend to put emotion on the back burner. This can make them seem cold, distant, or unaffectionate. They don't like cuddling or overt and cloying displays of affection. They don't like someone treating them as though they were helpless or needy or "cute."

Art tells the story about how he had just finished giving a series of talks for a marriage-preparation class. He was impressed by the young couples' overt displays of affection — holding hands, kissing, and snuggling throughout the many hours of lecture and instruction. Later, as they went on their evening walk, he took Laraine's hand in his. Concerned, Laraine immediately inquired, "Is your arthritis acting up?"

Cholerics tend to view affection as a bonus, once all other important business has been taken care of. They love to solve problems and hate to linger . . . on anything! But they are also quick learners; once they understand how important affectionate words and actions mean to their spouse, they are usually willing to try — because they want to succeed and have a strong marriage. Point out to the choleric that affection and empathy help a marriage succeed and flourish, and he'll make a mental note to strive to be more affectionate and empathetic. "Emotional investment" and "working together to achieve success" are models that will appeal to cholerics, provided there is no other impediment.

The active choleric (especially one who is married to a more reticent spouse) will need to understand how an overbearing and driven nature can inhibit the areas of life that require time, delicacy, gentleness, and vulnerability (such as personal intimacy). He may need to be convinced about the importance of lingering over a romantic dinner, turning off the Blackberry, and just talking and relaxing in an intimate way, sharing what is on his heart.

The Temperament God Gave Your Spouse

The choleric parent

As the head of a household, the choleric wants to lead the family, but it can sometimes feel like command-and-control rather than leadership. One choleric dad we know says that, when it's time for everyone to head off to Mass, he warns the kids: if you're not in the van on time, we're leaving without you! He's not kidding. (Cholerics don't make idle threats.) But this dad says that he has had to leave someone only once, and *voila!* Lesson learned!

As parents, cholerics can run the risk of becoming drill sergeants — believing that too much affection or empathy makes kids "soft," weak, or ill-prepared. Cholerics like to pull themselves up by their bootstraps, and wonder why anyone else would need warm fuzzies to motivate them. A choleric parent may struggle especially to understand a phlegmatic child: why isn't he doing more; why is he so quiet? Is there something *wrong* with that child? (No, he just isn't like you!)

A choleric parent needs to be aware that small children (especially those of certain temperaments) need affection, gentle encouragement, and time in order to grow and mature. Sometimes the choleric parent wants the entire household to march in lock-step to his tune of goal-setting and achievement — on the double! Two choleric dads we know (both entrepreneurs) told us that they can never relax as long as they don't see a sense of urgency and commitment to action — from their employees, their spouse, and their kids. They will keep on demanding and motivating until they see it.

It can be a challenge for the choleric to see things from another point of view, and to understand that other temperaments don't have the same sense of urgency and direct style of communication that they do. Children can teach their choleric parents patience, humility, and flexibility, especially as the family grows larger. One choleric dad we know had to give up his goals of having his oldest son follow in his footsteps into a military academy when the young man's less-than-stellar GPA made this goal unattainable. He discovered that his son had many other talents and aspirations, and he adjusted his own sights accordingly.

It is important for choleric parents to remember to express unconditional love; our children should know they are loved, even when they aren't little mini-me's. It was a moment of revelation when our oldest daughter went away to college and told her mom that she didn't argue all the time with her roommates about philosophy and theology . . . because she wanted to *keep* her friends!

The choleric at prayer

We see all around us marriages destroyed by lust, anger, selfishness, jealousy, domination, and even hatred. But the Church reassures us that Christ himself comes into our lives — as part of our marriage — to give us the strength and grace we need to have a happy and fruitful marriage. Spouses will be able to live a sacramental marriage by "following Christ, renouncing themselves, and taking up their crosses."[7] As St. Paul tells us, "Husbands, love your wives, as Christ loved the church and gave himself up for her."[8] Temperament plays a part in the sacramental life of our marriage, just as it does in our daily life in the temporal sphere.

Without adequate human and spiritual formation, the choleric can go from energetic and confident to overbearing, prideful, controlling, and dismissive. A choleric's natural confidence may turn boastful, his forthrightness may seem rude, and his bold action may lead him away from God.

[7] CCC, no. 1615.
[8] Eph. 5:25.

The choleric's goal-driven nature can be used for good or for ill — the key is focusing on the *right* goal. St. Paul persecuted the early Christian community, "breathing murderous threats against the disciples,"[9] but once converted, he became the greatest apostle. The independent and opinionated choleric often finds it difficult to submit his will to another (for example, to his spouse, to Christ, to the Church, or to a spiritual director). He must continually fight against his tendency to pride, which leads him to prefer his own will, to think he is always right, to become angry with others, and to want to be in control when he really ought to let go.

But once the choleric realizes that he must grow in humility, in obedience to God's will, and in charity and solidarity with all men — for "none of us lives for himself"[10] — he will begin to make great strides in his spiritual life. When he learns to dedicate time to prayer and reflection, he can bring his abundant energy and strong will to Christ's mission.

If you're a choleric, ask yourself: Am I willing to let my spouse have the last word on occasion? Or do I drag out arguments to the bitter end, simply because I have to win? Am I willing to put aside my agenda once in a while, to let my partner have a say in the direction our family is going? Do I sometimes stoop to belittling remarks or sarcasm, just to reinforce my dominant position? Am I willing to ask for help? Do I see meekness as a weakness, or a necessary virtue? Do I sincerely try to understand and empathize with my spouse?

---

[9] Acts 9:1.
[10] Rom. 14:7.

The Four Kinds of Spouses

YOUR SOCIABLE SANGUINE SPOUSE

*Tigger told Roo (who wanted to know) all about the
things that Tiggers could do.*

"Can they fly?" asked Roo.

*"Yes," said Tigger, "they're very good flyers, Tiggers
are, Stornry good flyers."*

"Oo!" said Roo. "Can they fly as well as Owl?"

"Yes," said Tigger. "Only they don't want to" . . .

"Can Tiggers swim?"

"Of course they can. Tiggers can do everything."

A. A. Milne, *The World of Pooh*

Your sanguine spouse is the life of the *partay!* He is talkative,
fun-loving, optimistic, generous, and enthusiastic. He places a high
priority on relationships and enjoys hosting, entertaining, volunteering, and networking. He connects with children — probably
because he's a big kid himself. Always up for something new, he
loves a spur-of-the-moment adventure — whether traveling to a
new city, meeting new people, or discovering a new idea.

On the down side, he can be impulsive, attention-seeking,
scattered, and forgetful. He always prefers something new and exciting to the same old, same old (especially the boring details), so
he is restless and easily bored. His cheerfulness and optimism are a
great boon to a marriage — unless there is a genuinely serious issue to face. The sanguine wants to look *only* on the bright side,
which can sometimes frustrate his spouse, who would like, on occasion, to bring up difficult or somber topics. Because the sanguine
believes everyone should *love* him, he can be rather thin-skinned
when it comes to criticism. Unless they have a secondary choleric
temperament, sanguines either turn a deaf ear or become very discouraged and are tempted to give up altogether.

The Temperament God Gave Your Spouse

Taken to an extreme (or without good formation), this temperament can be given to hedonistic pursuits. His active senses will lead him toward all that is glamorous and glitzy about the world. Combined with his sanguine impulsivity, this tendency can wreak havoc with his bank account! Indeed, sanguines tend to be well-liked and amusing socially, but can try their spouses' patience — especially when it is time to settle down, maintain a solid work ethic, and attend to the more routine details of raising a family.

Still, the sanguine is usually a creative and energetic breadwinner, willing if necessary to take on unusual projects. On the job, he likes to be a flurry of activity — that may or may not be entirely productive. He loves to have a finger in every pie (sometimes to the annoyance of his less flamboyant colleagues), and he will charm and inspire his coworkers with his creativity and Big Plans — although sometimes he won't have the perseverance, attention to detail, or time to carry them all out. Of all the temperaments, sanguines are the most likely to job-hop; sometimes they just can't resist the allure of new opportunities, friendlier people, or more money just around the corner!

Can you imagine a sanguine librarian? It's not easy to picture that bouncy, talkative, bundle of energy sitting sternly behind the stacks, tackling the Dewey Decimal system. But sanguines (like Tigger) are confident that they can do anything. One sanguine we know parlayed her teaching experience and love of kids and books into a job as a school librarian. As the principal once remarked, "Yours is the noisiest library I've ever been in." (No wonder!)

The sanguine in love

The sanguine can be demonstrative and sensual, but also can move quickly from hot to cold. The sanguine wife will be warm and generous, emotional and impetuous . . . but then in a flash she can be just the opposite. When a sanguine turns off, she is really *off*. A sanguine husband needs to cultivate the virtues of temperance and self-control, or he may be easily led (or misled) by superficial physical attractions or the emotions of his heart. Both male and female sanguines are eager to please their loved ones, but can also unintentionally mislead others with their innocently flirtatious and open manner with the opposite sex.

It is good to remind the sanguine that love is not primarily a feeling, but is a function of the *will* (otherwise, Christ could not have commanded us to love!). Love requires patience and perseverance and a willingness to seek deep understanding of self and spouse, which do not come naturally to the sanguine. But, when these long-haul skills are combined with the sanguine optimism and good cheer, the marriage can flower.

The sanguine parent

Kids love a sanguine mom or dad. The sanguine typically relates well to his own children and to their friends. He has a natural, easy manner and is rarely punitive or repressive. He is flexible and entertaining, always participatory. Sanguine parents volunteer abundantly at their children's schools, going beyond ordinary lunch duty or bake-sale donations to driving the activities bus, renovating classrooms, substitute teaching, and coaching. They are very hands-on, restless if they're not involved.

But like most temperamental qualities, these can be a mixed blessing. When serious child-raising problems arise, the sanguine parent may be tempted to gloss over them, hoping that his usual big smile, pat on the back, and optimistic outlook will do the trick. When more is required, especially deep soul-searching on the part of the sanguine himself, the solution may be harder to come by. It may also be a struggle for sanguines to connect with a quiet, reticent (usually melancholic) child. Wanting to cure him of "antisocial" behavior, a sanguine may take over and "speak for" a shy child, forcing him into social situations — usually with counterproductive results. A sanguine parent can overwhelm a more introverted child to the point that the child gives up even trying to develop his own personality.

A sanguine parent with a sanguine child, on the other hand, can be a dynamically destructive duo, if they are not careful to temper their tendencies to impulsive fun and people-pleasing. You read about some of the more inept ones on the news; they're the ones going to jail for serving alcohol at their teenagers' birthday parties!

But law-abiding sanguine parents can get into trouble too. Partly sanguine Laraine once accompanied sanguine son Sam into a situation of great temptation — the Verizon store. All those shiny new phones! Unfortunately, only Art and Laraine were due for an upgrade. No problem. Laraine made a quick call: "Art, do you want a free upgrade? You can get a Razor!"

"I don't need an upgrade. My phone is just fine," replied phlegmatic-melancholic Art. He was trying to set an example of temperance and frugality. Sam and Laraine gave each other high fives. *Excellent! Sam gets Art's upgrade, and we both get new phones!* Yet this was tantamount to Jacob's stealing Esau's birthright. Poor Art won't qualify for an upgrade for another two years!

The sanguine at prayer

The pure sanguine temperament is remarkably forgiving, relationship-oriented, and supportive — a recipe, you might think, for self-giving in marriage! Ah, but remember, no single temperament defines perfection in this fallen world. There is that little sticking point, the Cross.

Sanguines are wonderfully generous, open and forgiving . . . until the going gets tough. That's when the sanguine goes shopping! Or out to eat, or to the movies. If you are the sanguine spouse, are you willing to listen — really listen — to your spouse, especially when the topic is uncomfortable or depressing? Are you overly dependent on what people think — to the point that your spouse feels neglected? Can you remain joyful throughout illnesses, financial difficulties, and other trials? Can you set aside your need to be the center of attention and focus on your children and spouse?

A sanguine's spirituality is often found most visibly in acts of charity; remember, he likes to be with people and to help them. But his eager generosity and willingness to help can disguise an unwillingness to persevere in difficult projects, to "put out into deep water," as Christ enjoined the sanguine Simon Peter.[11]

Thus, the sanguine must recognize his tendency to superficiality and to vanity, and resist the temptation to perform good works for the attention or just out of an overdeveloped desire to please. These factors can conspire to keep the sanguine busy with many apparently good undertakings, yet without the merit and other spiritual benefits that come from reflection, and from having the underlying intention of doing everything out of love for Christ. With the help of a spiritual director to guide him in prudential choices and in developing an interior life, the sanguine can fight these tendencies, and discover a deeper sense of joy and accomplishment when he learns to meditate on Christ's words: "He must deny himself and take up his cross daily and follow me."[12]

[11] Luke 5:4.
[12] Luke 9:23.

YOUR METICULOUS MELANCHOLIC MATE

*"Have you all got something?" asked Christopher Robin
with his mouth full.*
*"All except me," said Eeyore. "As usual." He looked
around at them in his melancholy way. "I suppose none
of you are sitting on a thistle by any chance? . . . It
doesn't do them any Good, you know, sitting on them,"
he went on, munching. "Takes all the Life out of them.
Remember that another time, all of you. A little Consideration, a little Thought for Others, makes all the
difference."*

A. A. Milne, Winnie-the-Pooh

The melancholic spouse is sensitive, introspective, and self-analytical. He loves order, beauty, quality, and quiet. The high-minded melancholic approaches marriage seriously, and will often be a perfectionist who strives for a strictly organized home. Because melancholics tend to be more comfortable with their own thoughts than with socializing, they can sometimes appear aloof or distant. They feel deeply, but cannot always express themselves right off the bat. Perceptions take a while to register with melancholics, but once a reaction occurs, it can be quite vehement. Like a fine wine, the melancholic needs time to reach his full potential — but when he does, it will be a fully realized one.

In relationships, the melancholic can sometimes appear to be pessimistic or even negative, demanding, and overly critical. More often than not, he seems more attuned to his own feelings and sensibilities than to those around him. Loved ones who are subjected to the melancholic's high standards and intense scrutiny often find this sort of perfectionism oppressive and, depending on their own temperament, may give up trying or become angry and rebellious.

Employers appreciate the melancholic's ability to delineate clear boundaries as to how much, and when, and by whom work is done. Melancholics are careful and exacting workers, and take seriously the noble tasks of providing for a family financially and for creating domestic order. Their perfectionism can be a mixed blessing, though — leading to great achievements or paralyzing with scrupulous self-doubt. Melancholics can become accomplished professionals or unfulfilled and underutilized malcontents; they can create clean and beautiful homes (they make committed and rigorous homeschoolers too), or they can let stress and fear of failure lead to domestic torpor.

The melancholic in love

Melancholics are romantics. They may not appear to be such — the flashy Don Juan or Lola is more characteristically sanguine. But, deep down, they long for the ideal love; they read poetry and relish classic romantic films. A melancholic male may be more likely to express his affection in terms of tenderness and lingering romance than men of other temperaments, and thereby score points with his wife. Provided their idealism doesn't degenerate into self-pity, bitterness, or jealousy, melancholics have a great capacity for expressing faithful love and affection for their beloved soul-mate.

This can make for a beautiful and intense courtship and a passionate married life, but over time it can also cause trouble in a marriage, when their fallible human spouses fail to live up to critical melancholics' romantic dreams. A melancholic man may find it hard to deal with the effects of time and family stress on his spouse and their marital relationship; a melancholic woman may find she requires everything to be absolutely perfect (flowers, wine, spouse's good behavior, engaging conversation, babysitter, feeling "in the mood" . . .) for her to engage in romantic intimacy. A melancholic wife, more than any other temperament, is likely to subscribe to a concept like "holy sex": wanting physical intimacy to feel significant on a higher, spiritual plane . . . and not being interested when it isn't.

The sensitive melancholic can also be easily hurt or offended by what appears to be a rebuff or lack of interest, even when it's wholly unintentional. He can become upset if his spouse doesn't do what *ought to be done* — and his spouse *should know* what that is, even if it is not explicitly stated! Here, communication is key: a melancholic would be wise to remember that his spouse is not a mind-reader! It is better to let your spouse know about your feelings, your desires, and your needs than to brood about an insignificant remark or perceived lack of responsiveness.

The melancholic parent

Like cholerics, melancholic parents will have a tendency to want to control their children, whereas sanguine and phlegmatic parents will be more likely to be controlled. Although kids may think that they would prefer the latter to the former, there are drawbacks either way. Melancholic parents' sense of order, predictability, and consistent rules will ensure that their children feel safe and secure, as well as reinforce strong morals, personal responsibility, and their Catholic faith. Melancholic parents have a row of perfectly behaved children in the front pew at Mass and a four-year-old who will answer "to know, love, and serve God" on cue, when quizzed on the *Baltimore Catechism*.

But what if one of the children is a squirmy, distractible sanguine, a stubborn choleric, or a daydreaming phlegmatic? The melancholic parent, faced with disorder in the ranks, is tempted to deal unduly punitively with the miscreants who dare to act like, well, children. Discipline and high standards are important, but melancholics must be careful that rules and strict order do not become oppressive. Children are notorious for making abundant mistakes, messes, and being ignorant! A melancholic's high ideals and impatience for mistakes can be trying on other adults, but they can take an even bigger toll on children — because children are inherently *not there yet*. Rather than building virtue, particularly fastidious and exacting melancholic parents can inspire in their children — depending on their temperament — open rebellion, sneaky disobedience, or hopelessness.

Along similar lines, it's sometimes difficult for melancholics (who value all that is good, beautiful, and true) to understand a child's curiosity (especially a sanguine child) about pop culture. One melancholic mom we know is entirely baffled by the fact that her thirteen-year-old daughter seemed to know all about Jamie Lynn Spears, all the lyrics to *High School Musical,* and the latest Hollywood gossip — when she isn't even allowed to watch television in their home. Was her daughter reading *Tiger Beat* magazine on the sly? It sometimes happens, however, that a parent's absolute ban on all things media inadvertently fuels the child's attraction to the forbidden fruit.

The melancholic at prayer

One might imagine that the reflective melancholic would have the advantage over the other temperaments when it comes to the spiritual life. They do have a strong inclination toward the interior life; they have a built-in longing for noble ideas and a correspondingly deep sense of sin. But they have characteristic weaknesses, too. They have to fight against inflexibility, a tendency to Pharisaism, and a scrupulosity that can undermine the simplicity of their faith.

The Temperament God Gave Your Spouse

A melancholic spouse needs to be on guard that the perfection he seeks is the perfection of love — not *perfectionism*. The latter can lead to navel-gazing, self-absorption, and even scrupulosity — none of which encourages a healthy sense of self-giving needed in a marriage. Fight against this temptation by growing in love and humility, following Christ, who "did not come to be served but to serve."[13]

In marriage, melancholics have to be on guard against an especially subtle form of spiritual pride: assuming that they're spiritually more advanced than their spouse. This can be especially devastating to a marriage when a melancholic wife assumes spiritual headship of her family.[14] A melancholic wife may be tempted to fall into the role of matriarch of the family, the "queen bee" around whom everything and everyone must revolve. Consider the model of the Virgin Mary, who followed her husband's lead even though she alone (of all human beings who ever lived) could rightly say that she was more perfect than her husband! Yet, how many times have we heard (or uttered) the complaint, "My husband is spiritually less advanced than I am!" It must strike her poor spouse as quite condescending and even prideful, yet it is uttered in all sincerity, from someone who feels she has a more intimate relationship with the Lord.

---

[13] Mark 10:45.

[14] Because, as God has ordained it, the husband is the spiritual head of the family. This has nothing to do with being a bully or a macho tyrant, as John Paul II wrote in *Familiaris Consortio* (no. 25), but everything to do with St. Paul's admonition that men must love their wives as Christ loved the Church. In God's divine order, the man is the spiritual head of the family. Thus, it was imperfect St. Joseph (not the Immaculate Conception) who received the news from the angel that the Holy Family must flee to Egypt.

One melancholic wife we know used to attend so many holy hours that her husband began to resent the Catholic faith! She would leave him alone every Friday night, not realizing how this made him feel more alone and more resentful of her deep spirituality. They discussed this issue from both sides, and eventually she came to understand this and changed her scheduled holy hour to a time when her husband was not at home, thus leaving more time to be available to him and to join him in his interests. We are each called to help our spouse grow closer to the Lord, and this does not mean growing wonderfully "perfect" all by ourselves!

If you are a melancholic, ask yourself: How often do I meditate on God's providential care for me and my family? Do I count my blessings and reflect in gratitude for all the good things God has given me? Do I resist those discouraging, critical, and despondent thoughts so they do not take root in my soul? Am I able to look at the "big picture" and refrain from dwelling on the potentially discouraging details that threaten to steal my joy?

YOUR PEACEFUL PHLEGMATIC PARTNER

*"I see now," said Winnie-the-Pooh. "I have been Foolish
and Deluded," said he, "and I am a Bear of No Brain
at All."*

*"You're the Best Bear in All the World," said Christo-
pher Robin soothingly.*

*"Am I?" said Pooh hopefully. And then he brightened
up suddenly.*

"Anyhow," he said, "it is nearly Luncheon Time."

A. A. Milne, *The World of Pooh*

The even-tempered phlegmatic spouse loves harmony, peace, and cooperation. He is humble and dedicated, supportive and never ostentatious. Solid, dependable, and affable, the phlegmatic spouse values security and family traditions. Phlegmatics are the most patient of all the temperaments, rarely get bored, and are cautious (yet not fearful): which makes them dependable providers, methodical and hard-working even when performing the tedious tasks that home life demands.

Phlegmatics are the backbone of our society, with their homebody natures, their traditional values, their strong moral sensitivity, and their inherent sense of loyalty. They are not flashy or reckless or sensational, out to make a dramatic splash in society or a major impact on history. Practical and solid, they take slow, methodical steps toward unpretentious and unselfish goals.

But, the phlegmatic can sometimes value cooperation so much that he fails to assert himself or take charge when necessary. At work, he can tend to be overly patient with the status quo, remaining in a lower-level job for lack of assertiveness; at home, rather than provoke confrontation, he would rather absorb the blame for family problems himself. He is easily discouraged and can lack self-confidence, making him prone to distancing himself as a means of self-protection. Out of a fear of interpersonal conflict, the phlegmatic spouse can minimize or overlook interpersonal problems, even while being painstaking about the solution to mechanical ones.

The phlegmatic in love

Phlegmatics are not flamboyant wooers; chances are they won their spouse's heart by their gentle goodness, not through overt romantic gestures. Fittingly, they're typically easygoing, undemanding, and discreet about physical intimacy. They prefer not to talk about sexuality, but are generous and self-giving partners. Phlegmatics can be excellent listeners, with a natural tendency to being empathic and understanding. They are also likely to keep the drawbridge down, and not hold grudges that would impair intimacy.

On the other hand, phlegmatics are the most likely to neglect their appearance — figure, physique, dress, and hygiene — thinking that "it doesn't matter" to their spouse (plus, they're just less prone to vanity). Since phlegmatics are quite satisfied with straightforward and down-home romance, they might miss their spouse's hints in favor of a little more pizzazz in the romance department — say, candles and soft music, sweet-talking, poetry, or a romantic movie.

Just this past Valentine's Day, a big, gray pickup truck drove up to our house and a woman hopped out carrying a clipboard. Laraine's first thought was, "Uh oh, it's the homeowners' association writing us up for not promptly removing the trash cans or for failing to take down the Christmas lights!" Instead, it was a flower delivery — the last thing Laraine expected from phlegmatic Art on Valentine's Day!

Yes, phlegmatics sometimes need to boost their expressivity if they want to engender romantic feelings in their spouse. At a talk Art recently gave at a local parish, a young couple gave a testimony about the temperaments. One evening, phlegmatic "Nick" told his young wife, "I am *so happy* being married to you."

"Hold that exact expression," she commanded and ran to get a mirror, which she held up to his face.

"Does this look to you like *so happy?*" Nick had to admit that his bland expression did not match the emotion he intended to convey.

The phlegmatic parent

Phlegmatic parents are easygoing and patient with their children. They enjoy the simple things of life: playing baseball in the backyard, reading the favorite bedtime stories over and over, and walking the crying baby in the middle of the night (that is, if they were already awake). They are soothing and comfortable, like an old shoe, and children appreciate this. But because the phlegmatic has a hard time being demanding or insistent, he may leave discipline to the more assertive spouse, yet he may also resent the spouse (especially if the phlegmatic is a male) for taking over. A phlegmatic parent may be puzzled or even concerned if he happens to have a choleric child, and he may not realize the need to keep a tight leash on a sanguine child, until it's too late.

Still, children will generally benefit from the stability that a phlegmatic parent projects. The phlegmatic's even temper, long-suffering patience, and capacity for withstanding abuse also make him ideally suited to raising teenagers!

The phlegmatic at prayer

Father Conrad Hock, the great Catholic expert on the temperaments, wrote little about the phlegmatic temperament in his

1934 classic, *The Four Temperaments*. He noted that the phlegmatic "has no ambition, and does not aspire to lofty things, not even in his piety." Surely his greatest temptation is to be content with the status quo, spiritually as well as humanly. *I go to Mass on Sunday; what else do you want?*

However, we believe that the natural humility of the phlegmatic should be considered one of his greatest strengths. A choleric may undertake great and arduous works, a sanguine may preach charismatically, and the melancholic may aspire to the heights of contemplation — yet, none of this is even possible without humility. As St. Teresa of Avila wrote, "Humility is the foundation for the spiritual life."

That same quality benefits the phlegmatic within the sacrament of marriage. A phlegmatic spouse is quite naturally self-giving, willing to acquiesce to preserve peace, to set aside his own needs and desires in order to meet the needs of his family. Like a camel, he can go a long while without being in the limelight or having his own preferences catered to. He can carry his crosses without complaint. Yet, there are some occasions when the true cross means stepping outside your comfort zone, taking a stand, and facing up to conflict. This can be a hidden, more difficult cross for the easygoing phlegmatic. If you are a phlegmatic, ask yourself: Am I willing to stand up for the sake of my family and my faith? Will I defend my spouse if necessary? Am I getting just a little too complacent in my spiritual life? Am I afraid to ask my spouse how I can grow spiritually and in our marriage?

Part 2

∞

The Temperaments and Communication

"[T]here can be no love without suffering,
because it always demands an element of self-
sacrifice, because, given temperamental differences
and the drama of situations, it will always bring
with it renunciation and pain."

Pope Benedict XVI, God and the World

∞

Have you heard the old joke about the three keys to marriage being communication, communication, and communication? It's not all that funny — but it's *very* true. The way we talk to our spouse, especially when it comes to thorny issues or personal problems can either help . . . or hinder. We can either encourage or discourage further discussion. Sometimes we communicate so poorly that we end up starting a fight.

Would you ambush your boss in the elevator to ask him for a raise? This is why we need to develop good communication skills.

Each of the temperaments has certain communication strengths and weaknesses. In the next four chapters, we present some real-life challenges couples have faced in their marriage (names and situations have been changed). We also present some tried-and-true communication *skills* that can help prevent and resolve some of these communication problems.

We want our marriage to be an "intimate community of life and love." But to build this community we need some practical tools, such as empathy, the softened start-up, the underlying positive, being open to influence, being specific, and expressing overt appreciation for our spouse. When we become proficient with these communication skills, we are actually growing in virtue — for these good habits of communication are difficult to attain, requiring self-control and the tempering of our immediate natural reactions. With these new skills (virtues) and with Christ as our firm foundation, our marriage will not only weather the inevitable storms of life, but will also be a sign of Christ's love in the world.

Chapter 3

∞

Connecting with a Choleric

"He comes, leaping across the mountains,
bounding over the hills."
Song of Songs 2:8

∞

Choleric Michael and his wife, Kay, have been married for twenty-five years. Once a teacher, Kay feels blessed to have been able to stay at home with the kids, because Michael turned out to be an entrepreneurial genius who started three successful companies. Now in his mid-forties, the dynamic and intense Michael exudes confidence and energy. At work, he is known for his keen intellect, strong will, and commitment to excellence. He attacks household repairs with the same vigor and focus as he would a marketing plan. Typical of cholerics, Michael is enthusiastic for big things, confident in his delivery, and rather dismissive of opposing viewpoints.

Proven right 98.5 percent of the time

As Father Conrad Hock puts it, cholerics' "natural virtue is ambition."[15] They can be powerful motivators and are driven to achieve excellence — for themselves and their families. But they are often so focused on the goal or outcome that, at times, they can be accused of rolling over people.

It's not that cholerics are heartless; they just are more intensely focused on the mission — often more so than on other people's feelings. This can overwhelm those with more delicate temperaments. If your spouse is choleric, you may find yourself at times comforting those who were inadvertently trampled underfoot. Our pastor says that he once worked as a "fireman": when he

[15] Hock, *The Four Temperaments*.

served as an associate pastor, he spent most of his time putting out the fires started by the choleric pastor!

It doesn't help that cholerics have an innate drive to be — as Rush Limbaugh proudly promotes himself — "proven right 98.5 percent of the time." Unsurprisingly, this can make people of other temperaments feel as if they're being bulldozed. Our friend Eileen says that she loves to study the temperaments, because it helps her understand her choleric husband. She chuckles when she says, "I used to get upset about how my husband is such a know-it-all and always assumes he is right! But now I realize that it is just part of his temperament, and I can laugh about it . . . And, of course, he usually *is* right!"

Because they assume they're right, cholerics just *have* to argue when someone ventures to disagree. Try not to take it personally. Young cholerics sharpen their baby teeth on debates, grabbing hold of an opinion like a puppy playing tug-of-war with a sock. Sometimes it's best just to let them tussle. Parents of all temperaments tend to be alarmed when faced with argumentative children; they assume that the child is "disrespectful" of their authority, or worse, is an incipient anarchist. But with a choleric child this is often not the case.

One day, twelve-year-old Lucy (a choleric, like her mom) was studying herself in the mirror with a worried expression.

"Mom, I think my head is shaped weird," she said.

"No, it's not," Laraine replied without looking. "Your head is supposed to look like that."

"But look at the way it's sort of rounded, behind my ears," she insisted.

"What are you talking about? It is *supposed* to be round behind your ears!" Laraine retorted impatiently. "If your head went straight back behind your ears, you'd look like a Martian!"

"Martians' heads don't go straight *back* behind their ears," argued Lucy, instantly diverted from the topic at hand. "They go straight *up* from their heads, like this." Lucy demonstrated.

"Not *those* Martians," Laraine argued in reply. "The *other* Martians; the ones whose heads go straight back from their ears!"

"What are you two arguing about?" interrupted sanguine Sam, who had been listening in bemusement. "Neither of you has ever *seen* a Martian!" Which was true, but for two cholerics, hardly the point.

Cut to the chase

A choleric's natural argumentativeness is the key to understanding his spousal communication style. Extraverted cholerics do not shy away from discussing controversial topics, even those touchy marital issues involving finances or parenting. Rather than putting things on the back burner to simmer, they prefer taking out the "big spoon" to stir things up. A choleric will rarely decide that some things are best left unsaid, or that a problem will eventually "fix itself."

Not only are cholerics prone to speaking up early and often, but they usually get *right to the point*. They waste no time "schmoozing" or "making nice," if it serves no apparent purpose. (This is how they get their reputation of "rolling over people" — they don't intend to be bulldozers, but they are busy and focused on the outcome.) Cholerics often find "processing" or "venting" to be a waste of time. They eschew complaining, which they view as whining. One choleric entrepreneur puts it this way: "Never act like a victim — even if you *are* a victim."

When cholerics want something, they want it *now* — and that includes resolutions to interpersonal problems. Thus, they can quickly become impatient with "soft skills" such as empathic listening and using "I" statements (saying "I feel that . . ." rather than making a flat assertion). Cholerics like "straight talk," and thus tend to "shoot from the hip." (*If you get your feelings hurt by what I said, well, that's your problem, isn't it?*) They prefer facts to emotions and don't see any benefit in dragging out the process by talking about feelings. Such tactics may work well in politics or in large leadership roles, but don't always go over as well in an intimate relationship, where we are not just exchanging sound-bites, giving orders, or setting forth our platforms, but are seeking mutual understanding through a deep and enriching encounter with the beloved.

> Don't say, "You're making me angry . . ." Your spouse doesn't have that power. Only you can control your own feelings.

Cholerics have a tendency to interrupt other people before they've finished speaking. This is partly because they assume that they already know where the other person is heading and, in the interest of efficiency, want to "cut to the chase." This can make cholerics less-than-ideal listeners, and can lead to festering communication difficulties in a marriage, especially when the other spouse has legitimate complaints that aren't getting a fair hearing.

Conquering, not contemplative

These choleric tendencies — turning nearly every discussion into an argument, and then insisting on *winning* it — can be annoying (to say the least) to a spouse, who, depending on his temperament, may become resigned, hurt, or bitterly resentful. But in some marriages, that's not the main source of conflict with a choleric. Kay, whom we met at the beginning of the chapter, never found choleric Michael's style particularly offensive, for she was able to hold her own, without feeling overly defensive or having her feelings hurt. She was able to say with an appreciative laugh that Michael accomplishes three times as much as "ordinary mortals," and possessed the temperamental makeup and intellectual abilities to hang in there when he "drives" the family.

But there is something else that does bother her. "We just don't really talk," she confesses. "I mean, we talk about *stuff* — the kids' schedules, his projects, my CCD classes. But we don't talk about deep, *spiritual* things. We'll go out, just the two of us, but he never really opens up. He's a master provider, but I need a *spiritual* soulmate." Over the years of their marriage, especially as she became more spiritually sensitive, Kay slowly began to detect areas in which she was not being fed. She and her husband were being intimate physically, socially, and intellectually — but not emotionally or spiritually.

Unless he has a large dose of sanguine as a secondary temperament, the choleric's emotional side tends to be less developed, which can make him uncomfortable in the interpersonal arena. This does not mean he can't be an accomplished conversationalist, for the choleric will master whatever skills are necessary to achieve success. However, he will be lacking a certain interpersonal *depth*, since expressing his feelings makes him feel vulnerable. He would rather argue with you about politics than reveal his secret fears or hopes. When a problem arises in the marriage, or when his spouse is expressing a lot of emotion, his first reaction is to solve the problem as quickly as possible (without necessarily taking into consideration his spouse's feelings), or (worse) to be dismissive, cold, and domineering. Clearly this approach does not usually harmonize with family life, and his lack of empathy can drive his spouse and children away.

In the past five years, Kay had experienced a deep spiritual conversion, growing in her faith and her relationship with Christ. She really wanted to share this with Michael, but felt that they just weren't on the same page. For example, when Kay suggested that they attend a spiritual retreat especially for married couples, Michael snorted derisively, "I don't have time for that stuff! You go!" He didn't notice how this hurt Kay's feelings, because he was already busy with the next project. Prior to her own spiritual reawakening, it hadn't been so apparent to her, but now Kay was left recognizing the spiritual chasm between them, and with the realization that her husband, for all his talents, wasn't comfortable with deep, sometimes murky, interpersonal topics.

The care and feeding of cholerics

Finding a solution to this problem was no easy task for Kay and Michael. It can be difficult to "re-train" a very stubborn and opinionated choleric, because he typically doesn't think he needs to learn anything (or anything he hasn't already identified as need-to-learn). Cholerics are fiercely independent and figure they can solve pretty much anything themselves. And if you try to go head-to-head with a choleric, you will likely lose (unless you're also a choleric, in which case, you will butt heads).

The trick is convincing the choleric to *want* to undertake learning a new skill or to grow in virtue. When a choleric discovers *for himself* the need for growing in empathy and learning healthier ways of communicating, he will quickly put his abundant energy into the new task. But confrontational tactics such as humiliation or harsh criticisms only alienate him. Even when the choleric is roused to anger and obstinacy, his spouse should remain calm, and help him learn to cool off, before any problem or criticism is addressed.

When the choleric is suitably calmed and treated with respect, his driving ambition can be *directed* toward greater personal and spiritual depth, toward holiness and zeal for souls. As Father Hock reminds us, "even a very proud choleric can easily be influenced to good by reasonable suggestions and supernatural motives." In fact, he points out that many great saints were choleric; for the choleric can be consumed with a spiritual fire so powerful that it brings many souls to heaven. But first he has to be convinced of the worthiness of such a goal.

After Kay had brought up the issue, calmly and respectfully, Michael came to admit how Kay had changed after her spiritual renewal — becoming less argumentative and more attentive to *his* feelings. Even though (as he finally confessed) he was a "spiritual slacker," Kay had never made him *feel* like one. Realizing that despite being highly successful on the surface, his interior life was practically nonexistent, Michael agreed to follow closely as Kay modeled interest in the interior life, and began sharing with him excerpts from her spiritual reading. But she also *challenged* him (something any self-respecting choleric can step up to) to seek excellence, both in relationship with his family and in his walk with God.

> You can challenge a choleric; just don't be disloyal.

Because Kay always maintained respect and affection in bringing her concerns to her husband, and was always fiercely loyal to him (a critical need for cholerics) throughout, Mike let down his guard and opened himself up to her (and God's) loving influence. He was able to respond to the challenges of learning new communication skills and giving the interior life the high priority it deserves. He was on his way to becoming a more virtuous man, a better disciple of Christ, and a true emotional and spiritual soul-mate to his wife.

Standing up to the choleric

One major key to marital success, and one that we'll return to often, is to understand, appreciate, and respect your spouse's temperamental differences. At times, this can mean granting certain behaviors and tendencies a wide and generous amount of tolerance. We're not called to change the way our spouse is made, but to love him — and help him perfect his nature.

But there are times when temperamental tendencies get out of hand, and these are not to be merely tolerated. In the case of the choleric, in fact, this can be quite destructive. It's not charitable to "indulge" the worst aspects of the choleric temperament, putting up with constant overbearing behavior, for instance, while hiding behind the demeanor of the dutiful, obedient spouse. There are situations when the truly charitable thing to do is to speak up.

Dominican Father Emmerich Vogt tells the story of the "control freak" husband who would admonish his beleaguered wife while she swept the floor, "You missed a spot." That woman might mistakenly view such treatment as a "cross" she's meant to bear, but in truth, her silence doesn't honor the marriage sacrament by helping her spouse grow in virtue and charity. In fact, the truly sacrificial and charitable act would be to speak up and say, "Here's the broom; you take care of it. It is good enough for me."[16]

Pope Benedict XVI wrote, "Fraternal correction is a work of mercy. None of us can see himself well, see his shortcomings well.

---

[16]Father Emmerich Vogt, O.P., "Detaching with Love": http://www.12-step-review.org/index.html.

So it is an act of love, to be a complement to one another, to help each other see one another better, and to correct each other."[17] Our sacramental marriage is the means by which we grow closer to God and bring *each other* to heaven. Salvation is never meant *for me alone*, but we are for each other instruments of grace.

I've made up your mind

In marriages where only one partner is a choleric, it's typical for him to lead and the non-choleric spouse to follow. So long as the choleric does not abuse his "power," both partners will likely be happy with the situation. In fact, their complementarity is probably what initially attracted them to each other: the high-powered choleric husband relishes coming home to his easygoing phlegmatic homemaker, for example, who, in turn, appreciates the choleric's drive and decision-making ability.

One scatterbrained sanguine we know is always grateful that her choleric husband reins her in when she impulsively embarks on yet another home-decorating scheme or over-commits herself to volunteering at church and school. He models for her how to "just say no" and gives her guidelines on setting priorities and sticking to a plan. In turn, her spontaneity brings a sense of fun and adventure to their partnership. In a healthy marriage, what usually happens over time is that both spouses not only appreciate each other's temperament, but they begin to grow in virtue as well: the phlegmatic learns to initiate, the melancholic becomes more decisive, the sanguine controls his tongue, and the choleric learns empathy and patience.

[17]Reverend Peter John Cameron, O.P., ed., *Benedictus: Day by Day with Pope Benedict* (San Francisco: Ignatius Press/Magnificat, 2006).

In marriages where a choleric wife is married to a non-choleric husband, the situation may require a bit more delicacy. Given the typical gender roles of the female as "nurturing/passive" and the male as "controlling/active," a choleric woman may appear disproportionately or unbecomingly commanding. It can be very tempting for a strong-willed, driven wife simply to take charge of the whole family and its direction, leaving the husband in the dust. One choleric woman we know is the director of a medical clinic; she also volunteers at her kids' school *and* coaches a sports team! Women with such strong personalities need to be very careful that they do not inadvertently harm their marriage by not meeting their husband's critical need to be respected and even admired.[18]

Another choleric wife complains that her husband is too "passive" when it comes to disciplining the children. She criticizes her spouse for not living up to his role as "spiritual head of the family." She claims that she has to do all the heavy lifting when it comes to making sure the children do their homework and say their prayers. He objects that his wife reacts too quickly; he *would have* gotten around to solving the problem, if she'd given him half a chance! Plus, he doesn't always agree with her about her disciplinary tactics. What she views as passivity (because of her temperament) he views as being patient! He thinks that she reacts too quickly, becomes too easily angered, and that she needs to step back a little.

Once again the choleric would do well to understand and respect the very different — but equally valid — ways in which people of other temperaments are hard-wired.

---

[18]Willard Harley, *His Needs, Her Needs: Building an Affair-Proof Marriage* (Grand Rapids: Revell, 2001).

Communication skills for cholerics

Because of their take-charge style of communication, cholerics may be more prone than other temperaments to provoking clashes. When they learn to use good communication skills, however, cholerics can achieve more success in their relationships. Here are two that can be especially useful for cholerics to practice:

> St. Francis said we should seek first to understand. This is empathy.

• *Empathy* is never easy, because it entails going outside of oneself, putting oneself in another person's shoes. But it can be a special challenge for the self-possessed choleric, who tends to seek the quickest, most direct solutions, to practice *empathic listening*. Cholerics may also confuse empathy with active listening (your spouse says, "I am really annoyed right now," and you reply, "You *seem* really annoyed right now"). But active listening is very cognitive and can become mechanical and impersonal, whereas empathy emphasizes tuning in to two critical elements: the speaker's *feelings* and *motives*. As the communication expert and marital psychologist Bernard Guerney puts it,

INSTEAD OF	TRY THIS
"*Now* what's wrong?"	"You seem upset. Do you want to talk about it?"

the empathic listener tries "to be attuned to wishes, desires, motives and feelings — including some that may not have been verbalized by the speaker — and to reflect those in response to the speaker."[19]

[19] Bernard G. Guerney, Jr., Ph.D., Keynote Presentation at the Smart Marriages Conference, July 2002.

Empathy is a way of practicing self-giving, of overcoming self-ishness. Empathy means I empty myself of my issues, concerns, goals, and responses, and focus totally on the other: on how he feels, or on what he has to say (and why). "Thus, after the act of listening, I am another man, my own being is enriched and deepened because it is united with the being of the other," wrote Pope Benedict.[20] This is crucial in our marriages — part of the radical self-giving that Christ calls us to.

• Another communication technique that can blunt the choleric's sharp edges is the *softened start-up*. It *eases* into an issue by working up to it through other topics, or by inviting the other to engage in the conversation at the time of his choosing, rather than putting him on the spot. Cholerics, of course, don't mind taking a direct hit: "Just tell me what you want, now!" they will say. But for other temperaments, the softened start-up is often necessary in order to be successful: the phlegmatic's slower response time, the melancholic's tendency to self-criticism, and the sanguine's reluctance to address any subject that might bring him down can all lead to discouragement and withdrawal if they're approached with too much directness. But that doesn't mean you *never* get to the issue; we remind cholerics that the softened start-up is not beating around the

> **INSTEAD OF**
>
> "Dinner isn't ready yet? What were you *doing* all day?"
>
> **TRY THIS**
>
> "The kids have so many activities going on right now that it must be hard to get anything else done! Is there something I can do to help get dinner on the table?"

[20]Cameron, *Benedictus*.

bush, but is, rather, setting things up so that the discussion will be productive and a resolution achieved.

Beginning with the pronouncement that "we've got to talk right now *or else*" ushers in defensiveness even before the topic is mentioned! But a softened start-up allows the other person to enter *freely* into the discussion at his own pace, even to choose when he will discuss it — thereby avoiding that feeling of being attacked and having to defend himself, which will keep a choleric's spouse from fully participating in the discussion and prevent the issue from being successfully resolved.

COMMUNICATING WITH A CHOLERIC — CHEAT SHEET

Responds	Quickly, intensely, with lengthy duration
Sociability	Extraverted; energized by social situations, but less talkative than the sanguine
Recognizable traits	Natural leadership and take-charge attitude; strong will; confident, opinionated, decisive, and competitive
Focus	Highly focused
Wants to know	The bottom line, the essentials, the action item
Makes decisions based on	Logic, expediency, and the goal (is willing to bend rules in favor of a successful outcome)

Needs	Loyalty, control, appreciation, independence; to be in charge
Weaknesses	Thinks his view is the best, the only right one; lacks empathy; fails to seek counsel; individualistic; bossy
During interpersonal conflict	Tends to blame others or get angry; insists on being right or wants to "fix it" immediately
Is annoyed/upset by	Slowness, inefficiency, disloyalty, distractions, whiners, complainers
Pays attention to	Power, organizational chart, bottom line, success, goal
How to deal with the choleric	Treat with respect and admiration; allow him to take charge in appropriate ways; help him grow in empathy by showing him how it will help him become more successful

Chapter 4

∞

Schmoozing a Sanguine

"My lover is radiant and ruddy;
he stands out among thousands."
Song of Songs 5:10

∞

Tony is a friendly, back-slapping, charismatic, big-talking sanguine with a knack for conceiving exciting new ventures. But his big dreams never seem to pan out. Tony's lack of attention to detail, overly trustful nature, and tendency to gloss over problems have resulted in several financial fiascos — a tough roller coaster for Tony's wife, Jennifer, and their family to ride.

Tony says Jennifer is being pessimistic and a downer when she tries to caution him about getting involved in yet another risky business venture. His feelings are hurt when she doesn't "trust" him. But after two decades of hearing the refrain, "*This* time we're really going to make the big time!" they had very little savings, and Jennifer was fed up. When Tony and Jennifer came into counseling, Jennifer was determined to go back to work and Tony was dead-set against it. "I don't want you working outside the home when we have young teens who need our attention at home!" he objected. "But we need the money!" she cried, frustrated.

But the real problem was not her potential job. That was only the latest in a long series of arguments. The real problem was that Jennifer had slowly been losing respect for her husband; indeed, she righteously felt that Tony did not *deserve* any respect, because he had been so foolish on so many occasions. When they were newlyweds, Jennifer had been aglow with pride for her ambitious, creative spouse. But after years of repeated failures (there had been some successes, as well, but now Jennifer was focusing only on the failures), she was discouraged and no longer supportive of new ventures.

Tony wanted to win her respect back, but didn't know how. He was feeling discouraged not only by his financial troubles but also because his wife no longer "believed" in him. He worried that she would lose even more respect for him if the family began to depend on her income.

As counseling progressed and the couple took a hard look back over the years, both realized that Tony's sanguine temperament had played a key role in creating the situation in which they now found themselves. Tony had always relied on his temperament's natural strengths, yet had failed to curb its corresponding weaknesses.

Born to run wild

The sanguine's fun-loving spontaneity, his talent for meeting people, and his enthusiasm for new adventures all tend to attract the more cautious or reserved temperaments. But over time, with the increased responsibilities of a growing family, house payments, and greater financial stakes, it can become tiresome. And when the weaknesses of the sanguine temperament are unchecked, as they were with Tony and Jennifer, it can lead to imprudent business decisions, over-spending, and a chaotic family life. With good reason is it said that money problems are a major source of and ongoing contributor to communication problems in marriage.

As Tony came to see how his unchecked impulsivity and guileless generosity had contributed to the financial disasters, he realized that he would have to make a change. He could no longer blindly follow the dictates of his temperament into imprudent and impulsive decisions. Meanwhile, Jennifer, with her more cautious nature, attention to detail, and deep sense of responsibility, could have been a big help — *if* Tony had only involved her more in the decision-making up front. For her part, Jennifer needed to realize that she had an important contribution to make to the family's economic destiny, and that she couldn't remain passive, letting the sanguine "run wild" with his grand schemes and then speaking up only to cast blame on him afterward. But rather than looking back, they needed to start afresh. They needed to see themselves as a team, and not as adversaries.

Counting our blessings

To do this, it was vitally important for Jennifer and Tony to maintain a high level of respect and affection for each other — "for better, for worse, for richer, for poorer." If Tony could be assured of Jennifer's unconditional love and respect for him despite his failings, perhaps he would not be so averse to her bringing in some extra income. If Jennifer knew that Tony respected her prudence and intelligence, she'd have been more confident in playing her part in making financial decisions.

> Your spouse is not a mind-reader. If you want him to know something, you have to say it.

Tony and Jennifer both also had to be reminded of the love they had at first[21] and of their commitment to the marriage. Jennifer recalled how Tony's enthusiasm and zest for life inspired her. She reminded herself how many long, hard hours Tony had worked on building a new business — all for the sake of their growing family. Tony needed to recall how much he enjoyed — and still needed — Jennifer's disciplined qualities, which had so attracted him in the beginning.

[21]Rev. 2:4.

Thus, Jennifer and Tony learned how to focus on and express what we call the *underlying positive*. This means trying to see your spouse and your marriage through Christ's eyes. When we are angry or feeling hurt, we tend to forget about the good things and focus only on what went wrong. Sometimes we let the negative feelings build up, or we stifle our complaints for so long, that negativity threatens to overwhelm the marriage, and bad thoughts about our spouse override any positive ones. Everything makes us further upset. We may lash out at our spouse or withdraw in silence, neither of which is a healthy response.

> An underlying positive is a good that is neither ruined, nor spoiled, nor discounted just because we have a problem to discuss. Choose to lead with love.

The antidote to this "negative override" is to express our concerns in a responsible, loving way (sticking to the present, not blaming) and to verbalize or acknowledge the underlying positive. If we can't think of anything specific, we can remind ourselves that our spouse cares about us and wants to do what is best for the family. We can focus on the things we are grateful for: count our blessings, concentrate on the good intentions of our spouse, remember why we fell in love. This is not "making something up" or putting on rose-colored glasses. Neither is

INSTEAD OF

"You're going to send us to the poorhouse, the way you shop!"

TRY THIS

"You have a great eye for decorating, and I love the way our house looks! But I'd like to sit down together and prioritize our spending."

it a flattering or buttering-up of our spouse. Rather, it's an acknowledgment of what has always been true and good about our marriage, but which has been obscured by the present difficulties. It is making the covert overt — openly appreciating our spouse.

Jennifer might express the underlying positive like this: "I'm really grateful for your willingness to shoulder the burden of supporting our family all on your own since we first had children. You are one of the most creative, talented men I have ever met." Jennifer can then express her concern about their financial situation. By beginning with the underlying positive, she diffuses potential defensiveness. The serious problems will still need to be addressed, but now Tony will be more open to doing so in a loving and constructive way.

Solving their financial difficulties was going to be a tough project, and it would take several years before their family would be out of debt. But with the firm foundation of love and respect, Tony and Jennifer could now begin to tackle their problems as a team.

Next time, you go alone!

You might think that communicating comes naturally to sanguines. They do love to talk . . . and talk . . . and talk. However, *good* communication requires give-and-take, and a full-on sanguine can sometimes miss the cues about when it's time to stop talking and start listening.

Sanguine Sally dragged melancholic Marvin to yet another dinner party. She used a little trickery to get him there, because Marvin was exhausted from a heavy travel schedule and was in need of some quiet time at home to recharge his batteries. Marvin had agreed because Sally had told him that one of his good friends (who equally dreaded such social functions) was going to be there.

Sally felt justified because she had been cooped up with the kids when Marvin was traveling, and she desperately needed some adult social time. "We won't stay long. I promise," said Sally. Marvin rolled his eyes inwardly, because once Sally got talking, it was hard to get away from *anywhere* quickly.

The dinner party lasted longer than Marvin would have liked, and Sally was in rapt conversation with someone who might have been her long-lost sister, but whom Sally had really only just met. Other guests were leaving, and Marvin wanted to slip out with the group. But Sally didn't see Marvin standing awkwardly alone, checking his watch and glowering at her. Marvin tried wandering back and forth past the two women deep in conversation, but they didn't even notice. He became more and more grumpy, and when they finally left and were alone in the car, he exploded: "You don't ever think about me; all you do is talk, talk, talk! That is why I never like going to these functions with you! Next time, you can go alone!"

> Sanguines need affection, attention, and activities — *with you.*

*Knowing when it's time
to curb our temperament*

This story illustrates why understanding our temperament is only the first step. We must accept our temperament as normal, and recognize how we have a tendency to react in a certain way. But we also need to know "when the expression of temperament can be free and spontaneous, when it should be curbed, and when it may be necessary to behave in an opposite direction."[22]

[22] Chess and Thomas, *Temperament in Clinical Practice*, 111.

Schmoozing a Sanguine

It was important for Marvin and Sally to understand and accept their differences in temperament and learn to put themselves in the other's shoes. Sally needed to recognize that when Marvin is away on travel, he spends a great deal of time schmoozing with his important clients — extremely taxing for an introvert. When he comes home to another social event, he is already on overload. When Sally talks too much, Marvin is tempted to retreat further into his melancholic shell — simply in self-defense! For his part, Marvin needed to understand that her being home with the kids didn't count for social time for Sally. Furthermore, that withdrawing in silence only provokes Sally to become even more garrulous, in an effort to draw him out.

If Marvin and Sally could take the next step, and learn not just the tendencies of their temperaments, but how to control them, over time they could learn to anticipate and even prevent problems from occurring. For example, knowing her capacity for socializing and Marvin's limits, Sally might give herself a deadline, or agree with Marvin on a time for spending at — and leaving — the party. Marvin, for his part, could agree that while at the party, he would extend himself a little more than usual, instead of stewing in a corner. Establishing these parameters ahead of time would make for a more cheerful ride home, and increase the likelihood that Sally and Marvin would attend future events *together*.

> **INSTEAD OF**
>
> "You paid *what* for that dress? Are you crazy?"
>
> **TRY THIS**
>
> "You look terrific in that outfit! I love how you take care of your appearance! But I am a little worried about our spending lately. I'd like to talk about our budget when you have some time."

Conflict is inevitable

Tony and Jennifer and Sally and Marvin were able to resolve their conflicts over finances, work, and socializing because they were willing to address the real problems. It sounds obvious, but it's not easy. More often, couples fight over things that are not the real source of conflict. They might have huge blow-ups or they might stew for weeks in silence, all over tangential (or completely unrelated) issues — proxies to the real, but unmentioned and un-addressed, problem. Some temperaments naturally lean into con-flict, and others are more conflict-avoidant (usually the sanguine will gloss over problems with false cheeriness). But no matter what their temperaments, until that real problem is addressed, both spouses will become ever more entrenched in their angry or hurt feelings, and in their self-righteous position.

John Gottman and his wife, Julie Schwartz Gottman, are world-renowned for their research on what makes marriages happy and what leads couples to divorce. One discovery they made shouldn't be too surprising: *conflict is inevitable in marriage.* As they write, "It's a myth that happily married people don't com-plain about each other's behavior. In fact, it would be ludicrous to expect two human beings to live together without complaints. We all have our idiosyncratic needs, desires, rhythms, and hab-its. And these needs are bound to collide, producing strong emotions."[23]

From a Christian perspective, this is because of Original Sin. Although we are created in the image and likeness of God, our hu-man nature is nonetheless subject to ignorance, suffering, death,

---

[23] John Gottman, Ph.D., and Julie Schwartz Gottman, Ph.D., *Ten Lessons to Transform Your Marriage* (New York: Crown Publishing Group, 2006).

and an inclination to sin.[24] Our relationships suffer as a result. We tend to be self-centered, to view *my* needs, *my* desires, and *my* views as ultimate. We can be selfish, ignorant, and weak-willed. So conflict, disagreements, and problems inevitably occur — in happy as well as unhappy relationships.

As Father Emmerich Vogt writes, "There is no such thing as a normal situation exempt from difficulties."[25] Marital happiness, therefore, comes not from avoiding problems, but in *dealing with them* in the right way. Indeed, the Gottmans found that when couples discussed a difficult or problematic topic, within *three minutes* there was a clearly identifiable pattern of communication that was predictive of the quality of their future relationship. Some couples became "gridlocked" by certain troublesome issues, making them miserable, whereas other couples were able to discuss similar problems with humor and even affection — even when the problems weren't completely resolved.

> For sanguines, a personal connection is not a bonus. It is critical.

Not only is it an illusion to think that a good marriage will be trouble-free: the Gottmans found that never raising problems or expressing a complaint is actually a problem in itself.

Constantly stifling your complaints is not a good idea. Doing so can cause you to hold on to angry, resentful feelings toward your partner. You may develop "negative override," where your bad

---

[24] CCC, no. 405.

[25] Vogt, "Detaching with Love." This does not mean the situation is hopeless, for we can place our hope in Christ's redemptive love; rather, we should accept the fact that difficulties will occur and we can prudently develop skills to handle them and trust in God's grace.

thoughts about your partner and relationship overwhelm and override any positive thoughts about them. You may start to stockpile your grievances, keeping track of each offense your partner commits. You may distance yourself emotionally to avoid the pain, or else lash out. Meanwhile, your offending partner, who rarely hears a negative word from you, is in the dark.[26]

There is an alternative to stifling our grievances in the one extreme, or exploding after "stockpiling" them in the other. The answer is to complain (that is, raise issues) in a healthy way: respectful, clear, specific, and immediate.[27] As Christian couples, we are working together to grow in holiness — we are a team.

Getting a sanguine to face up to problems

Art was worried about our son's grades. He noticed several Cs on the interims and told his partly sanguine wife that he didn't think the school was working out. Sanguine Laraine characteristically looked on the bright side: they were only interims! Besides, Sam had just broken his collarbone and missed several days of school.

You may notice that, at this point, neither of us had yet constructively addressed the problem or come up with a solution! That's because we gave into characteristic temperamental temptations: the melancholic, to globalize even small concerns, and the sanguine, to re-cast problems in a positive light.

Indeed, sanguines tend to flee from negativity. Their sunny temperament insists on looking on the bright side of all potential problems. But this optimistic and effervescent attitude is sometimes perceived as superficiality or putting on rose-colored glasses.

[26]Gottman, 25.
[27]Ibid., 26.

Sometimes sanguines can be rightly accused of sticking their head in the sand or of sheer naïveté. The non-sanguine spouse may begin to feel that he is the only one who takes anything seriously — whether finances, discipline, or marital issues. In a marriage, this sanguine tendency can interfere with necessary communication when it becomes a habitual refusal to recognize and delve into serious problems.

The sanguine temptation to gloss over problems and to look on the bright side can irritate spouses of other temperaments as well (unless both spouses are sanguine!). The non-sanguine spouse will often feel forced into being the "bad cop" — whether it means disciplining the kids, trying to stick to a budget, setting limits to fun activities, or making sure the homework is done. And, if there are some serious marital issues to address, the non-sanguine spouse will wonder how he can even begin to address them! He may wind up keeping these problems to himself — letting them build up until one day he explodes in anger, hoping to finally make the sanguine understand how serious the problem is.

> **INSTEAD OF**
>
> "Why am I the only person in this family who can balance the checkbook?"
>
> **TRY THIS**
>
> "I really could use a hand with the finances this month. Can I show you how I've got the bills organized?"

When we finally discussed the situation with our son's grades more rationally, we both realized that we needed to temper our instinctive reactions. It was good that Art wanted to address the problem, but it would be better to focus on the *particular* situation (interim grades), instead of taking the general doomsday approach. By avoiding generalizations ("nothing is working out!")

and sticking to the present ("let's see what we can do to bring up these grades"), we were able to tackle the issue without becoming defensive.

For her part, Laraine realized that as painful as the discussion seemed to be, it was necessary and constructive. She forced herself to take a hard look at all the factors involved, to really listen to all of Art's concerns, instead of coming up with quick fixes and easy solutions that only scratched the surface. With both of us working now on the same page (instead of working at odds), we could turn our attention to how best to help our son.

Communication skills for sanguines

Where the (likewise extraverted) choleric can be a poor listener because he thinks what *he* has to say is always right, the sanguine struggles with listening because he doesn't want anything too deep, serious, or involved to darken his sunny world. Sanguines would rather try to talk you out of your bad mood or throw themselves into a hundred activities than patiently sit and listen to your problems — especially if the sanguine himself is part of the problem! If you are a sanguine, work to overcome that tendency, and become a better listener (your spouse will thank you!) by practicing the following communication skills:

• Practice *listening with your mouth closed.* Hear out what your spouse has to say without interrupting or interjecting your own thoughts or feelings. Then, after a suitable pause, repeat back to him what he just said, and ask whether you've correctly understood his point. Only then may you insert your own comment!

• Train yourself to make others the center of attention by running *marital diagnostics:* periodically asking your spouse (especially if your spouse is of an introverted temperament) whether there's anything that's bothering him, or any difficulty he'd like you to try to delve into. Be prepared to listen with your mouth closed, and then try not to immediately "cheer up" your spouse or downplay his concerns. This will not only build up the virtue of selflessness, but will also get you into the habit of giving problems their due weight rather than reflexively making light of them.

• Sometimes sanguines can interrupt or begin talking before they think about how to say something more gently. So, as for cholerics, we recommend that sanguines practice the *softened start-up* (see page 60). This will help you ease into a touchy topic, bring up a problem, or express an unhappy feeling in a neutral, less accusatory fashion. Harsh start-ups begin with criticism, blaming, or contempt, and almost always result in defensiveness or withdrawal. To avoid these, try using the softened start-up, which might include *talking personally* ("I feel . . .") and also might *ask permission* to discuss the topic, to keep from "ambushing" your partner.

COMMUNICATING WITH A SANGUINE — CHEAT SHEET

Responds	Quickly, intensely, with short duration
Sociability	Extremely sociable, extraverted, attuned to what is going on around him (especially people)
Recognizable traits	Enthusiastic, lively, open, talkative, social, creative, fun-loving, generous; greatly values relationships and people

Focus	Easily distracted, especially by externals; can be easily attracted to something new
Wants to know	Who will be there? Will it be fun? Are you going with me? Are you happy?
Makes decisions based on	Interpersonal connections; what other people think; who is involved; whether people will like them
Needs	Attention; fun activities together; positive interactions; flexibility; doing things together; joy in life
Weakness	Can be hasty or superficial; tends to flee from negative; scatterbrained; exaggerates; a finger in every pie; people-pleasing; lack of follow-through
During interpersonal conflict	Wants to look on the bright side; avoids negativity; may skim over problems or pretend everything's fine
Is upset/annoyed by	Lack of attention; negativity or harsh comments, indifference or hostility; problems; lack of fun/love in life; anything boring or unpopular
Pays attention to	What people think about them; how things look; what is popular; what others think or do; what is "out there"

How to deal with the sanguine	Take a positive approach; do things together; express your love and affection for him; help him to set priorities and not over-book; help him to follow through; hold him accountable

Chapter 5

∞

Meeting Minds with a Melancholic

"My dove, my perfect one!"
Song of Songs 5:2

∞

Colette is a sensitive melancholic married to a forceful and decisive choleric. In the early years of their marriage, Colette often had her feelings hurt. She felt that choleric Dan was comparing her (unfavorably) with other, more confident women (notably his high-powered sister), and sometimes she even suspected that he considered her just a wee bit crazy.

"*Am* I crazy?" Colette asked. "Dan tells me I am so insecure and oversensitive, and that he would *never* compare me with his sister. So why do I have these thoughts?" When Dan came home from work, he would often find the house a mess and Colette frazzled and desperate for help with caring for the toddler and the baby. Colette would complain about how overwhelmed she was — she couldn't even get around to shopping for dinner! Dan would then say something like, "I don't understand why it's so hard for you. My sister Janet has five kids, and she also has her own business! I don't see why you can't just get a simple meal on the table!" Colette then felt that not only was she a whiner; she was also a failure!

As a sensitive and thoughtful melancholic, Colette takes most things very seriously and is very deeply affected by thoughts and impressions. Lack of order in her daily surroundings makes her feel out of control and discouraged, yet she's not able to solve problems efficiently and quickly (*too* quickly, she sometimes thinks) like her choleric husband.

Father Conrad Hock compares the reaction of the melancholic to the hammering of a post into the ground; with each successive blow, the post is driven deeper into the ground, until it is nearly impossible to remove it.[28] With each perceived "failure" on Colette's part, the post of her feelings of incompetence was driven further into the ground. She felt herself falling farther away from her image of the "ideal" spouse, and this distressed her deeply. Some melancholics (those who have a secondary choleric temperament) tend to react by redoubling their efforts to maintain control. Others (those who are partly phlegmatic like Colette) might react by becoming progressively overwhelmed and discouraged. In general, melancholics react to the fear of losing their ideal by criticism — either turned *outward* on those around them, or *inward*, upon themselves (and sometimes *both!*).

Colette says she wanted to hear Dan say, "I understand how tough it is for you right now, and how overwhelmed you feel. But I know you can do it. You're just having a rough time right now." But instead, the cold and commonsensical advice he gave her just made her feel defensive and incompetent. Choleric Dan, sensing her helplessness (and not knowing what else to do), would just *take charge*. He'd roll up his sleeves and get the toddler to join in on a "let's count how many toys we can pick up in five minutes" game — making Colette feel ashamed that she hadn't thought of it. She'd spend all day at home, feeling as if she was accomplishing nothing, then he'd come home after a hard day at work, clean up the downstairs in five minutes, and entertain little Greg.

Soon Colette's sensitive nature was questioning her very competence as a wife and mother. Her house was a "mess" (in her own estimation), the children weren't cooperating, she didn't have time to cook nutritious meals, and she feared she would vent her

---

[28] Hock, *The Four Temperaments*.

pent-up anger and frustration on the kids. She didn't have her sister's energy or talent for quick solutions; instead, she would muddle through one task after another, frustrated and unhappy. The classic melancholic strives to attain a high degree of excellence. Unfortunately, the fast-paced life of a mom with small children underfoot is quite the antithesis to the melancholic *beau ideal* of order and excellence.

Turning molehills into mountains

Colette was at a critical juncture for the melancholic: how to handle daily disappointments in a healthy way, for melancholics are prone to sliding down a negative slippery slope. They may start with "I let the day get away from me" and then slip downward toward "I am doing a lousy job today," then "I always do a lousy job," to "I must be a lousy mom." And finally, "I am a terrible person!" Or, the melancholic may turn to an even more globally despairing thought: "My marriage is terrible!"

Whoa! Put on the brakes! To stop sliding down the slope, Colette needed to separate reality from her own thought process. Was she in fact doing a lousy job? Was she really a lousy mom? No, she wasn't. But her thoughts were causing her to feel frustrated, moody, and even depressed.[29] Colette needed to learn that it was her *temperament*, and not the objective situation, that was making her so despondent over Dan's comments and leading to her own feelings of inadequacy. Only then could she begin to take practical steps to alleviate her frustration.

---

[29]Cognitive therapy teaches us that self-defeating thoughts can negatively impact our emotions and our behavior, even leading to depression. Cf. Keith Dobson, Ph.D., *Handbook of Cognitive Behavioral Therapies*, second edition (New York: The Guilford Press, 2001).

Colette also had to realize such spirals of self-criticism were foreign to Dan's choleric nature. Dan would never think to waste a moment's energy "drowning in self-pity"; if he saw a household problem, he wanted to solve it and get on with life. He also didn't care whether the house was "perfect" — so long as he came home to a happy wife and kids, and a warm dinner! Even if she told herself that she was failing to meet Dan's (or his sister's) standards, she was really failing her own: each time slipping deeper into self-recrimination and ultimately self-pity.

The melancholic's introversion makes him deeply thoughtful and meticulous, but it can also leave him less aware of others' reactions (while ultra-attuned to his own). Sometimes this leads to the creation of an "alternate universe" inside his head, where children obey without question, where spouses are mind-readers, and where arguments are debated and won. When a melancholic spouse comes home to his chaotic family; youngsters screaming, "Daddy!"; the dog escaping out the door to terrorize the neighborhood; and the entryway cluttered with backpacks, shoes, and sports equipment, he wants to run away and hide in his library with his friends, the books. Or he leaves to work out at the gym.

> The tendency to generalize increases when we're angry. It takes discipline and practice to stay focused and specific when upset.

When he's finally alone, he conducts an argument in his head with his wife. By the time he resurfaces, he's in a fine stew and delivers a state-of-the-union speech indicating all that is wrong with the household. His unsuspecting family is mightily offended and wonders where the foul mood came from. His wife angrily points out that the baby has an ear infection, the toddler threw up, and all the neighborhood children wanted to play at our house today. "When did you expect me to tidy up the house?" she demands. The baby begins to cry. Soon everyone is in an equally bad mood.

The way life ought to be

All melancholics must remind themselves that everything does not need to be "perfect." Indeed, nothing *can* be. This is true right down to the mundane details of everyday life. Babies cry, milk spills, dogs bark, and moms don't always have time to clean the house. But even reminders can't prevent some melancholics from trying to make things perfect.

Laraine's melancholic mother strives to maintain a perfectly organized home, where *everything* has its proper place. One day, Laraine observed that her elderly mom was struggling to make her way to the sofa, turning her walker sideways to squeeze past the sofa table and the bookcase, inching her way past the two obstacles. When Laraine offered to move the furniture over a bit to make more room, her mom refused. "No, this is how the furniture is *supposed* to be!" Laraine commented that she'd hate to have to squeeze past furniture every day. "No, you wouldn't," insisted her melancholic mom. A melancholic wants everything in its place . . . and everyone should *like* it!

When the melancholic insists that things must be done just *this way*, their children and spouses often ask, bewildered, "What difference does it make?" It seems more fuss than it's worth. The furniture cannot be moved — even if everyone else must change their way of getting around. The children should sit perfectly straight at Mass (try that with toddlers); dinner must be served at 6 p.m., no later, no matter what the rest of the family's schedule is. In the melancholic worldview, there is a certain order to things, to which other people should simply adjust.

The constant litany of *shoulds* and *oughts* can take a big toll on the family. Melancholics have a way of "ruling the roost" in a subtle, unspoken fashion: casting dark glances, heaving heavy, disappointed sighs, or even experiencing physical symptoms when things are not going as they should. This can result in frustrated, angry, or discouraged kids and spouse. Depending on the temperaments of the spouse and children, reactions to the melancholic's drive for perfection and occasional intolerance of anything short can range from resigned helplessness to angry rebellion.

Be perfect . . . not a perfectionist

The perfectionist's demands can drive *him* crazy, too — just as it did to Colette. But when Christ said, "Be perfect, just as your heavenly Father is perfect,"[30] he did not mean, "Be a perfectionist." The perfection that Christ calls us to is the perfection of *love*, which leads us to holiness and friendship with God; but perfectionism, which is often an attempt to make up for low self-worth by impressing ourselves and others with doing things perfectly,[31] only makes everyone miserable. When perfectionism means being too-perfect-to-please, a melancholic's high standards can become a cross for his loved ones.

The three children of melancholic Monique will tell you just how discouraging this can be. "My mom never understood that I just wanted to hang out with my friends sometimes," said second-born Jude. "She expected me to study every minute so I could get into her alma mater. My older sister always did everything 'perfectly' — but she had no life!" Meanwhile Jude's mother was

---

[30] Matt. 5:48.

[31] A feeling of worthlessness should be addressed with the help of a professional therapist.

always criticizing him, his friends, and his pursuits. Jude began to be very discouraged about his grades, his goals in life, and even his faith. In reality, he was not a "bad" kid — he was just a typical sanguine.

Melancholics are sometimes perplexed by sanguines, because their reactions are 180 degrees different. Melancholics take things seriously; sanguines want to enjoy life. Building a warm relationship (whether spousal or parental) instead of being a commandant is a more effective way to motivate sanguines, but for some melancholics, this can be hard to understand and even harder to achieve, because it seems tantamount to lowering their standards.

> Seek the perfection of love — not perfectionism.

But the melancholic does not need to *lower* his standards; he needs to learn to how to "sell" his high standards. To do this, the melancholic first needs to *accept* others for who they are, and then *motivate* them to change. Motivating is often a foreign concept to the melancholic, for whom the very existence of high standards is motivation enough. *Everyone* ought to have the same high standards, says the melancholic. But this is not the real world we live in. If the spouse of a melancholic feels (or is made to feel by the melancholic's criticism) that he can *never* measure up, that the standards are impossibly high, then discouragement and often rebellion follow.

And so, rather than nag her sanguine son, and compare him unfavorably with the more-perfect daughter, melancholic Monique needed first to understand and accept her sanguine son's very different temperament, and that it was a gift from God. Only then could she begin to motivate Jude in a manner likely to produce results rather than rebellion.

That underlying positive again

Melancholics have the ability to persevere through trials as they pursue arduous and noble goals, but they often have to battle discouragement arising from daily commonplace irritations. If left unchecked, this discouragement can lead to depression, especially if the object of discouragement is oneself. One way to battle discouragement is to address one issue at a time (and not to globalize disaster at the first mistake) and to set more realistic goals. Along the way, it can help the melancholic to focus on the *underlying positive* (see page 68).[32]

Melancholic Monique, for example, needed to remind herself that Jude was overall a good kid who got decent grades, went to Mass every Sunday, and just needed a little extra motivation in the academic arena. Colette had to force herself to acknowledge that not only was she not a total failure, but she was in many ways a good wife, mother, and homemaker.

All of us must recognize how our thoughts impact our feelings, but this is especially important for the melancholic, whose tendency to introversion can lead to isolation and discouragement. The idealistic melancholic is likely to have developed a habit of focusing on what is *not* working — those aspects of his life that are falling short. This may contribute to a prevailing negative mood. But once we observe the connection between thoughts and feelings, we can seek to challenge pessimistic thoughts and to develop a new pattern of thinking.

For example, Colette might tell herself, "I think I am a lousy wife and mother, but really I am just having a tough day with three

---

[32]Bernard G. Guerney, Ph.D., *Relationship Enhancement: Couple/Marital/Family Therapist's Manual*, third edition (Silver Spring: Ideals, Inc., 2003).

little kids. Anyone else would, too." Or, the melancholic dad can remind himself (before he enters the door), "My wife has been home nursing two sick children, without a moment to herself." Then he can practice substituting positive thoughts for the negative ones: "I am doing a really good job with these three little children!" or "My wife is so selfless in her dedication to our children! I am so grateful to her!"

INSTEAD OF	TRY THIS
"I'm such an idiot!"	"I'm trying my best. That's what matters."

In Christian terms, this is "counting our blessings." When we count our blessings, we become more grateful, and thereby directly increase our joy. St. Paul (himself perhaps a choleric-melancholic) writes to the Philippians, "Whatever is true, whatever is honorable, whatever is lovely, whatever is gracious, if there is any excellence and if there is anything worthy of praise, think about these things."[33] By reflecting on what is honorable, lovely, gracious, and praiseworthy in our spouse and our kids (and ourselves!) we will become more capable of overlooking the smaller frustrating details that can so skew the melancholic's perspective.

> The softened start-up may seem to you like "beating around the bush," but your spouse doesn't experience it that way.

Once the melancholic has countered his negative thoughts and replaced them with gratitude and good thoughts, he can develop the habit of expressing his gratitude and his loving thoughts *aloud* — to his spouse and children. At first, it might seem awkward and

[33] Phil. 4:8.

even contrived, but your spouse's reaction will be the motivation you need to keep this up. Don't assume that *she knows I love her* or *he knows I am grateful for the work he does* — say it.

Studies have shown that happily married couples make *five positive comments* to every one negative![34] These couples have developed the *habit* of voicing loving thoughts. We must overtly express our positive thoughts about our marriage. A spouse may say, "She knows I love her because I work so hard" or, "Would I cook and clean the house if I didn't love him?" While it is critical to do loving things, it is also critical to express our loving thoughts. This is removing the bushel basket and letting the light of our love shine forth.

Communication skills for the melancholic

The purpose of self-knowledge is not navel-gazing or drowning in self-recriminations. Practicing a few communication skills can help the melancholic become more other-centered and less likely to provoke defensiveness.

• One communication technique that a melancholic can put to good use is to *be specific and avoid generalizations*. When we are angry, hurt, or experiencing pain, it tends to color everything: *"You never come home on time!" "You always leave a mess." "You never initiate sex." "You are always so sarcastic!"* Using terms such as *always* and *never* tends to kill communication. Two things immediately happen: first, our spouse will feel defensive (because the accusation is probably unfair) and second, we stop talking about the problem and instead focus on a rebuttal. (*"I remember one time I wasn't late!"*). Then we lose the opportunity to address and solve the problem constructively.

[34]John Gottman, Ph.D., *Why Marriages Succeed or Fail* (New York: Simon and Schuster, 1994).

Instead, we should be specific, focus on the present, and talk about one issue at a time. *"I feel really upset because I made this special dinner and you came home late!" "I really wanted you to return my call. Can we talk about that?"* In Corinne's case, instead of saying, "You *always* compare me with your sister!"

INSTEAD OF
"This place is falling apart!"
TRY THIS
"I really need help this weekend. Do you think you might have some time to mow the lawn?"

or *"Nobody* thinks I do *anything* when I am at home taking care of the kids!" she might say, "When you tell me how much your sister Janet gets done in a day, I feel as though you are criticizing me for what I do." Or, "I am really feeling discouraged right now about how messy the house is, and how much time it takes just changing the baby and entertaining the toddler."

• Reflect on (and express) the *underlying positive.* When a melancholic begins to focus on problems or to engage in self-pity, he may overwhelm himself and everyone around him with a sense of discouragement and gloom. Negativity is contagious. When overriding gloom threatens your mood or when you need to address a serious problem with your spouse, begin with the underlying positive. Leading with the underlying positive does not exclude the opportunity to address a problem; it enables the couple to address the problem in a more hopeful, cooperative fashion.

St. Paul notes that we should have no anxiety, but make our requests with thanksgiving![35] If your feelings are hurt because your spouse came home late yet again, remind yourself that he loves

---

[35]Phil. 4:6.

INSTEAD OF
"The kids will think you're an ogre, the way you yell at them all the time!"
TRY THIS
"I can tell that you're really worried about whether the kids are working hard enough on their school projects. I am, too. Let's talk about how we can help them get more organized."

you so much that he goes to work every day *for you*. Then tell him how thankful you are.

This might not come easy at first. But when the melancholic has developed a *habit* of acknowledging the positive things about his spouse and expressing loving thoughts, his spouse will be far more likely to respond in kind and charity will abound.

COMMUNICATING WITH A MELANCHOLIC — CHEAT SHEET

Responds	Slowly but intensely; a prolonged reaction, with intensity building over time
Sociability	Introverted; energy drained by social activities; needs time alone to recharge; is comfortable alone
Recognizable traits	Quiet, thoughtful, detailed, critical, high-minded, serious, sensitive, artistic, persevering, tends to "perfectionism"
Focus	Intense; inward; focused on detail; marked by persistence
Wants to know	More details and specifics; further information; what are the rules

Makes decisions based on	Principles, how things "ought" to be, the ideal
Needs	Support; help in initiating projects or social activities; to be heard and understood; order and quiet
Weakness	Slow to initiate; indecisive; can be critical and inflexible; will say no if pressed for immediate response
During interpersonal conflict	Tends to let problems build up and then will overstate or become awkwardly vehement and overly dramatic; tends to generalize negatively
Is upset/annoyed by	Lack of principles; being rushed into decisions; frivolity; lack of attention to detail; superficiality; disrespect for personal order
Pays attention to	The ideal; internal feelings and thoughts; past grievances; procedures; what is "right"
How to deal with the melancholic	Respect their rules, their quiet, their order, and their space; support them in initiating; acknowledge their valuable insight into problems; give them time to make a decision; ask what is on their mind

Chapter 6

∞

Fanning the Phlegmatic Flame

"Love is patient . . ."
1 Corinthians 13:4

∞

Phlegmatic Ben is a quiet, hardworking engineer, married for twenty-five years to his high school sweetheart, Annie. He had managed to put two of their six children through college and was unwaveringly supportive of Annie's avocation to homeschool the younger ones. Annie was grateful for Ben's solid commitment to the family and his steady fidelity to the Faith.

Annie was able to stay at home with the kids, although they weren't able to afford expensive vacations or fancy home furnishings. A typical phlegmatic, Ben never sought out more lucrative (but perhaps risky) jobs or aspired to top management positions. He was satisfied with his niche, so long as his work was respected and he received a steady paycheck. But increasing competition from younger, more technologically savvy engineers had forced Ben to work longer hours just to maintain his position. In fact, over the past couple of years, Ben had been feeling increasingly under pressure as he was passed over for promotions while his supervisor demanded ever-greater productivity. He no longer had time for home "fix it" projects, nor was he available to help with kids' homework; now he came home late from the office every night only to settle in front of the computer, catching up on emails and bills. He was even too tired to sit up late with Annie and chat or watch movies together, as they used to.

"We never talk anymore," complained Annie privately. "The house is falling apart, and I can't discipline the kids all by myself! Sometimes it seems as if Ben is sleepwalking through life." Annie knew how hard Ben was working, and the stress he was under at work, so she felt guilty complaining about him. Still, she thought, "If he would just talk to me about it, maybe I could help. But I just never know what's going on inside his head!"

A temperament of few words

Phlegmatics are almost always outwardly agreeable and cooperative, but not always very communicative. When our phlegmatic son was very young, we proudly — and anxiously — watched him swim his first hundred-meter butterfly at an invitational meet. We watched from the other side of the pool as his coach called him over to speak to him after the event. From that distance we could see the coach earnestly gesticulating, demonstrating strokes, and putting an arm on our son's shoulder, all the while Ray was dutifully nodding. Finally, when he came back over, we eagerly asked him, *"What did he tell you?"*

"I don't know," said Ray.

We soon learned that this short phrase is a hallmark of phlegmatics young and old alike. Perhaps it takes too much energy to come up with a response, perhaps their reaction is merely delayed, or perhaps they are stalling in order to find out what answer will be most acceptable to the questioner. Or perhaps they're trying to nap. When he was older, in an effort to solve this mystery, we quizzed Ray. "When you say that you 'don't know,' do you *really* mean, 'I know . . . but I don't want to tell you,' or perhaps, 'I'm pondering very deep and difficult concepts that cannot be satisfactorily addressed at the moment'?"

"No," replied Ray affably. *"I just don't know."*

If the phlegmatic is male, the problem can be compounded. It is said that women utter three times as many words as men; thus the taciturn phlegmatic can seem even more enigmatic to his wife. This is the situation that Ben and Annie faced. As long as Ben's energy was not being completely drained by the job, he had always been available to relax after work and chat. But now Ben was feeling stressed, using all his concentration (and his full quota of words) at the office; talking with Annie afterward only increased the unwelcome stress, because he sensed her disappointment with him. So Ben hid behind the computer or watched TV, and Annie resorted to nagging.

Phlegmatics invite nagging like flames attract moths. For not only do they avoid conflict, but also they tend to procrastinate — in more ways than one. Because phlegmatics don't like looking into the nebulous, unknown future, they're already prone to procrastination. But when, as so often happens, they agree to something they don't *really* want to do, that tendency can be amplified. They don't want to do it, they don't want to say no . . . so they just let it slide. In a marriage, this can lead to a cycle of nagging, in which the phlegmatic's spouse grows increasingly shrill and frustrated, and the phlegmatic increasingly withdrawn or defensive.

Phlegmatics will often resort to "okay" or "I'll get to it" to buy some time — intending to get to it . . . later. If the phlegmatic is married to a choleric or a sanguine (who expects things to happen *right now*), this can give rise to conflict. The non-phlegmatic may resort to harsh generalities in a misguided attempt to motivate: "You're so lazy!" or "You never *do* anything!"

Because phlegmatics are averse to interpersonal conflict, they would rather avoid a problem than deal with the pressure involved in facing it. As a result, a phlegmatic might put up with years of abuse on the job (and nagging in a marriage) rather than face the intensity of a direct conflict. Unspoken resentment builds inside the phlegmatic, which may culminate in stonewalling — the phlegmatic has had enough and refuses to budge — or else the dam finally breaks and all the interior frustration finally pours out.

Compliant, thy name is phlegmatic

Phlegmatics are more comfortable going with the flow, agreeing with everyone else, rather than risking the conflict that might result if they dared to state their own preferences. Thus, they often say things like, "I don't know," or "I don't care . . . whatever *you* want to do." This is a blessing to parents and a pleasant surprise on a first date, but can be stultifying over time. Any natural temperamental quality can become a drawback if not governed by prudence — even the phlegmatic's famed easygoingness.

Sometimes Jesus turned the other cheek, and sometimes he turned over tables. The phlegmatic, naturally inclined to peace-making, must learn to speak up for the truth even when it creates conflict. Christ himself said, "I have come to bring not peace but the sword."[36] *True* peace is a product of conformity with truth, not merely the avoidance of conflict. In a marriage, there will be times when the compliant phlegmatic will need to step up to a problem, instead of simply agreeing with his spouse (to make the problem go away) or avoiding the issue.

Even the easygoing phlegmatic can become upset, especially if the provocation is severe. If he'd been stuffing his feelings for a long time, it can be quite an explosion! This is what finally happened with Ben. He had put up with the stress of work combined with Annie's increasingly vocal accusations without ever acknowledging the toll this was taking on him. One day the simmering inside hit its boiling-over point, and he finally burst out in loud and demonstrative anger, shocking himself and Annie.

Ben had to learn to address his home and work problems as they happened, instead of continually putting his feelings on the back burner. But it took a while to convince Ben that facing

[36]Matt. 10:34.

problems was worth the anxiety it caused in him. Finally Ben and Annie sat down and had a long talk. Ben dug deep and found the courage and initiative he needed to communicate his worries about getting laid off, and to tell Annie how he really needed her support. Annie said that she'd never realized the weight that Ben had been bearing, but now that she knew, she would certainly give him more support.

Annie realized, too, that she had become rather complacent about having Ben so available after work, and she promised him that the family could shoulder more of the load right now . . . just as long as Ben promised not to shut her out anymore. Ben, in turn, promised to speak to their teenage son about pitching in (instead of leaving it all up to her). They came up with a plan to go out one night a week to a local pub to catch up with each other. Annie developed a habit of asking Ben, "Really? Are you sure?" whenever he would say that he was fine, everything was all right. She encouraged him, with gentle attention and support rather than confrontational nagging, to share what was on his mind and in his heart.

> **INSTEAD OF**
>
> "So now you're the cleaning Nazi?"
>
> **TRY THIS**
>
> "I'm sorry I left a mess in the bathroom. I know how hard you work at keeping our house looking beautiful. I'm going to try harder from now on to help out."

Annie also had to commit herself to remaining empathic and non-defensive when Ben did have a complaint. She told herself that if she *really* wanted Ben to be more communicative, she'd have to learn to be more patient and receptive of what he had to say. Sometimes having an uncomplaining phlegmatic spouse can leave us with an inflated idea of how much we're contributing to the marriage! If we really want a phlegmatic to speak his mind, we must be prepared to hear criticisms we weren't expecting, and to guard ourselves against reacting out of wounded pride.

As is the case with any virtue, the more Ben practiced being open and initiating, the easier it became, even though every once in a while, he still had a phlegmatic zone-out. Another great result was that these disclosures strengthened their marriage, because Ben and Annie were now talking to each other on a deeper level about their likes, dislikes, fears, dreams, and desires.

That ship has sailed

We have seen from the foregoing examples that phlegmatics are compliant and conflict-avoidant, and do not always express what is going on in their mind and heart. This tendency is amplified by the fact that, when phlegmatics *do* react, the response is usually delayed and lacking intensity; while others are flinging repartees, the phlegmatic is still puzzling over the question. It can also result in their being underestimated.

Art likes to tell the following story to highlight the differences between the phlegmatic and other temperaments, such as the choleric. When we go to a movie, as we are walking back to the car, Laraine immediately analyzes the movie we just saw: the plot, the script, the dialogue, whether Denzel Washington was typecast, whether the score suited the plot, and what the critics are likely to say about it. Laraine pauses for a breath. "What did you think, Art?"

"Well, uh, let me see . . . I'm not sure. Let me think about it," says Art.

The next morning, after Art has had his morning coffee, he has an insight into the movie. It is all clear, now. Art is ready to discuss it.

"Laraine, let's talk about that movie we saw."

"What movie?" asks Laraine.

This story highlights the fact that it is tempting to accuse the phlegmatic of moving too slowly, of not caring, or of having no opinions. In reality, the reaction just comes more slowly to him. It is not that he has no opinions or ideas; he simply needs time to process. The choleric, on the other hand, is known for his hair-trigger reactions. He makes his opinions, thoughts, and decisions readily known. By the time the more deliberate phlegmatic gathers his thoughts, the choleric's ship has already sailed.

The underestimated temperament

Unlike the choleric, then, who has his arguments lined up in advance, or the sanguine, who just enjoys moving his jaws, phlegmatics have to *think* before they speak. That delayed response combined with a lack of intensity and with conflict-avoidance can conspire to create in the phlegmatic the "perfect storm" of non-relationality.

The spouse of the phlegmatic may therefore be frequently puzzled: Why is he so underpaid? Why doesn't he try to find a new job? Is he ever going to notice the clogged drain? Doesn't he have any opinions? Doesn't she have any goals? Does he ever stick up for himself? Or (like the young wife in chapter 2 who held a mirror up to her phlegmatic husband's bland face): "Does it look like you're *happy?*"

This lack of expressiveness and tendency to underreact can lead to frustration and lack of fulfillment for the spouse of a phlegmatic, particularly when the husband is phlegmatic. His wife doesn't know how to motivate him and wishes that he would just step up and take charge. Over time, she may resort to criticizing (if she's melancholic), nagging (if she's sanguine), or taking over for (if she's choleric) the phlegmatic, making him feel hounded, misunderstood, and inadequate. This often leads (no surprise) to a deep lack of self-confidence. Besides avoiding the kinds of accusatory behavior that only drives him deeper into his shell, a spouse can encourage the phlegmatic to draw out his leadership abilities.

> Don't swallow your feelings. This only increases the likelihood that you will explode in anger later on, and make the problem worse.

Because they tend to be passive and slow to react, phlegmatics are often accused of laziness or of lacking leadership skills (even Father Hock said as much). But this, in our view, is a great mistake. In our view, any of the four temperaments can be excellent leaders, provided they have received the proper motivation and formation. St. Thomas Aquinas is thought to have been phlegmatic. So, too, is our own pastor, who just built the largest new church in the diocese (at a time when most people thought it couldn't be done, given the high cost of construction). And although we know little about him, it's possible that the great St. Joseph — with his silent ways, his generosity, forgiveness, obedience, flexibility, and dependability — was also phlegmatic.

In fact, the phlegmatic has many natural gifts that can contribute to excellence in leadership: a spirit of cooperation, the capacity to work with diverse personalities, diplomacy, level-headedness under pressure, and the ability to create harmony and teamwork. Perhaps phlegmatics' greatest gift is their natural humility; the ability to ask for help and to seek guidance is a key quality in leaders. The trick is to convince phlegmatics to take charge. Their natural preference is to work cooperatively as part of a team, but a phlegmatic is also naturally inclined to being a "servant leader" who leads quietly, but unmistakably, by example and hard work rather than by flamboyant words, charisma, or power.

You can increase your phlegmatic spouse's self-confidence and sense of self-worth by encouraging (with gentle, positive persuasion) the loving leadership that is appropriate to his or her vocation. Since they don't seek the limelight, most phlegmatics need a little gentle push to accept leadership responsibilities, but once they've done so, they can thrive. Remember, the best way to help your phlegmatic bloom is to be overtly appreciative and encouraging. And a little old-time flattery can't hurt!

Communication skills for the phlegmatic

As a communicator, the phlegmatic does have a lot going for him: natural humility, empathy, and cooperation. He is unlikely to ambush or nag his spouse. Nonetheless, there are a few skills and attitudes he might need to develop.

Remember, the phlegmatic's default setting is to ignore, to smooth over, to ride out the storm. But sometimes ignoring a problem doesn't work, and the phlegmatic knows he'll have to address it. This is a cross for the phlegmatic: confronting the bullies, asking the boss for a raise, returning the cold soup, saying "no thanks" to the telemarketers, spending Christmas at home instead of dragging the family to the in-laws. Most of the communication skills phlegmatics could stand to learn relate in some way to their need to stand up to problems and to address them more vocally.

> **INSTEAD OF**
>
> "All you do is sit in front of the computer!"
>
> **TRY THIS**
>
> "You're so good with math; I wonder if you could help Danny with his homework, since he seems to be struggling right now."

• The introverted phlegmatic tends to assume that the other person knows what he is thinking or feeling without dramatizing it. (In fact, phlegmatics tend to abhor histrionics.) Train yourself to *practice expression*: becoming skilled at using more, and more descriptive, words to convey your thoughts and feelings. Be conscious of your vocal tone and volume. And think about physical expressions, too: phlegmatic Art practiced raising his eyebrows and smiling with a big, wide grin, in order to convey upbeat enthusiasm. He took up the Italian method of using his hands when talking. It can be done!

But being more expressive also entails being *willing to disclose* what is in your heart or on your mind. Sometimes, it is simply a matter of saying out loud what is on your mind. Your wife walks across the room, and you think, "Wow, she looks great!" Instead of merely thinking it, say it out loud. Other times, when the content is disagreeable or raises the specter of potential conflict, being expressive will take more effort. Here the phlegmatic will need to step outside his comfort zone, forgoing human respect (which leads to agreeing for the sake of pleasing others or avoiding conflict), and exercise courage and prudence (knowing whether to opt for peacemaking or the sword).

> Acknowledging your spouse's feelings decreases defensiveness and paves the way for further communication.

• Art also found that the *underlying positive* (see page 68) was one of the more difficult — but important — communication skills he needed to acquire. The phlegmatic doesn't practice this skill, as, say, the melancholic would, to temper his tendency to be critical (because he doesn't have one), but to avoid giving his spouse no feedback at all. Believing your spouse to be aloof and disinterested can be potentially more damaging than being the subject of constant criticism. And as we said earlier, when your non-phlegmatic spouse encourages you to be more vocal, he may not immediately like what you have to say! The softened start-up (see page 60) can help cushion the shock of hearing you finally say what's on your mind.

COMMUNICATING WITH A PHLEGMATIC — CHEAT SHEET

Responds	Slowly, not intensely, with short duration
Recognizable traits	Easygoing, quiet, dependable, peacemaker, reserved, calm (especially in a crisis)
Sociability	Quiet, reserved, easygoing, introverted, well-liked by many
Focus	Can be unmoved by externals, but can be distracted by internal feelings, especially those of discomfort
Wants to know	Will everything go smoothly? Are people getting along?
Makes decisions based on	Relationships; what others think or want; cooperation
Needs	Harmony, especially in interpersonal relations; structure; respect and appreciation; time for relaxation; peace

Weakness	Can lack initiative; overly compliant; might not stand up for self; overly tolerant of status quo
Is upset/annoyed by	Interpersonal conflict, noise, chaos, intense or extreme behavior
During interpersonal conflict	Will take blame to avoid conflict; will outwardly acquiesce, but might internally withhold agreement; might avoid conflict altogether because anxiety is so acute
Pays attention to	What others think or want, cooperation, harmony, duty
How to deal with the phlegmatic	Encourage him to take charge; gentle reminders (never nag); give positive feedback and words of affirmation to build up his confidence

Chapter 7

∞

Opposites Attract

"What drives me to you
is what drives me insane."
Bob Dylan

"Love is not love
Which alters when it alteration finds."
Shakespeare, Sonnet cxvi

∞

After one of our talks at a "marriage enrichment" evening for couples, a young husband approached Laraine. "I think you just saved my marriage," he said. "I thought there was something *wrong* with my wife — but now I know that she is just choleric!" Then he added, a bit sheepishly, "And I'm the other one . . . the one you talked about second."

That would be the oft-neglected phlegmatic.

Because we ourselves are completely opposite temperaments (Art is a phlegmatic-melancholic and Laraine a choleric-sanguine), couples often come up to us after we speak about our temperaments to tell us that they are, too. Each time, it's further proof that opposites *do* attract, and that the most important factor in a happy marriage is not being of like personality. Rather, what seems to make marriages happy is when husband and wife share core values, and a commitment to the relationship — to honoring and respecting each other and meeting each other's needs.[37]

As we noted earlier, it is often the case that we befriend people who have similar temperaments, but we *fall in love* with those of opposite temperaments. We find their foreign characteristics intriguing and attractive: the quiet, introspective melancholic is drawn to the talkative, outgoing sanguine. The peaceful, non-confrontative phlegmatic seems made for the strong-willed, take-charge choleric.

But we also saw that what initially attracts can over time become a source of consternation, puzzlement, or even annoyance.

[37]Cf. 1 Cor. 7:3.

The Temperamuet God Gave Your Spouse

After the initial romance (during which time we're usually on our best behavior and most tolerant of the differences), the extraverted sanguine might begin to resent her introverted spouse's lack of social interests. The melancholic spouse longs for peace and quiet in the home and is sometimes embarrassed by his talkative spouse's antics. A choleric spouse becomes annoyed by the phlegmatic's lack of ambition and passivity, while the phlegmatic withdraws from the choleric's demanding and active lifestyle.

Florence Littauer, renowned speaker and author of *Personality Plus*, tells the story of her discovery that her serious, thoughtful, organized husband was not going to be very much "fun" as a spouse. While they were on their honeymoon, he informed her that she did not eat grapes "properly," and no longer could she decide on a whim that she wanted to get ice-cream; it had to be scheduled! (Once they came to appreciate their differing temperaments, their marriage thrived, and they remained happily married for fifty years, until his death.)

Understanding, acceptance, and respect — temperaments-style

When the honeymoon is over (literally and figuratively), and we begin experiencing conflicts over temperament differences, frustration over our spouse's foreign (to our way of behaving) traits may well register as annoyance. But the real problem is not so much that we become tired of our spouse's very different style of being and interacting. Rather, we begin to worry that what is important to us according to our temperaments (such as harmony for the phlegmatic or social interaction for the sanguine) will not be considered important by our spouse. And so we worry that our *vital emotional needs will not be met.*

But when we come to understand how temperament differences affect our relationship, we can let go of that worry and can move from a cranky posture of "she is so moody" or "he is too pushy" to a loving acceptance of, and respect for, our spouse's different natural inclinations and deep-seated needs. This mutual posture of confidence, acceptance, and respect forms the basis for the self-giving love between husband and wife that every marriage needs in order to thrive.

> Empathy feels "fake," you say? Well, we don't always give in to our feelings. I want to understand my spouse, even when I don't feel like it.

A word about acceptance: *acceptance* does not mean complacency, or putting up with sinful or bad behavior. It is not blindness to our spouse's faults, but loving him *despite* his faults. Acceptance is based on the realization that we are all afflicted by Original Sin, and we all have our own limitations. But it does not mean becoming a doormat. We love our spouse, faults and all, but we hope that, with God's grace, we both will grow in virtue. In fact, knowing that we are loved unconditionally is often a prerequisite for the willingness to make the changes necessary to do so.

Hand in hand with acceptance goes *respect*. I do not need my spouse to be *just like* me; I do need him to *respect* me — and the emotional needs particular to my temperament. If those needs seem strange or even annoying, he must realize (hard as it may be sometimes for a spouse of opposite temperament) that I'm not intentionally out to irritate him. Without understanding and acceptance, respect is impossible — and spouses will interpret each other's temperamental reactions in the worst possible light: as willful attempts to nag, annoy, or "push each other's buttons."

Just as acceptance doesn't mean we let our spouse walk all over us, respect doesn't give our spouse (or us) license to become a "temperament bully." If I accept and acknowledge my choleric spouse's innate need for control, I haven't given him permission to turn into a maniacal dictator, bludgeoning all who step in his path. If I'm a sanguine whose melancholic husband has learned to acknowledge my need for socialization, that doesn't mean I can turn our home into a three-ring circus of nonstop visitors and parties.[38]

Fortunately, though, this usually doesn't happen. In fact, mutual respect for temperaments tends to lead to the opposite effect, soothing emotional needs rather than inflaming them out of control. Indeed, our experience has shown that *lack of respect* is often what creates extreme temperamental behaviors: your spouse will "stick to his guns," determined to show you how he ticks and to prove to you that his needs are important.

Acceptance, however, is the first step. Acceptance makes it possible for us to act responsibly, in freedom. When we accept our spouse's temperament (instead of trying to change it to be like ours), we are showing him respect and unconditional love, which frees him to undertake the tasks of the world and to serve Christ with confidence and joy.[39]

---

[38] A single friend of ours once fretted that she would be afraid to date a choleric. Would he take advantage of her naturally agreeable nature and turn into a dictatorial ogre? This all depends on his character, not his natural temperament, which is in itself neither sinful nor evil. But a person who chooses to indulge his temperament's short fuse may very well cross the line into sinfulness. Such an individual may be said to have a strong temperament, but a weak *character*. It would be wiser for our single friend to date men of strong, good character — no matter what their temperament.

[39] Cardinal Ratzinger, *Introduction to Christianity* (San Francisco: Ignatius Press, 2004). He goes on to say, talking

CHOLERIC/PHLEGMATIC
The captain and tentative

Phlegmatic Luke was swept off his feet by Nancy, a beautiful and talented choleric. She, in turn, was attracted to his classic phlegmatic virtues: he was dependable, well-mannered, attentive, and humble. Her parents wanted to start planning the wedding immediately, because none of the other young men their daughter had dated had been as considerate and caring. Plus, he was a good Catholic.

Luke took up all of Nancy's favorite activities: escorting her to concerts, visiting with her friends, going on outings to art galleries and museums. He rarely spent time with his own friends anymore, and gave up video games. Meanwhile, whereas Luke was willing to forgo his own agenda in order to keep the peace and maintain harmony, Nancy was behaving in a rather typical strong-willed choleric fashion — stating her opinions and demanding compliance. When his friends accused Luke of being "a tool," he replied that being in a relationship required self-giving and sacrifice.

However, as time went on, Luke began to wonder: was he being truly virtuous, or was he simply avoiding confrontation? Passive conflict-avoidance is not the same, or as virtuous, as positive self-giving. How much of his "self-sacrifice" was simply a phlegmatic fear of making waves? How much of it, too, was due to a deep-seated insecurity, rather than the positive force of self-giving love?

about salvation: "The primacy of acceptance . . . alone makes it possible to do the things of this world in a spirit of responsibility, yet at the same time in an uncramped, cheerful, free way . . ." We believe that acceptance on the supernatural level also applies on the natural level, with our loved ones.

Here is an illustration of why self-knowledge is so important for growth in virtue, as the saints often remind us. Without self-knowledge, our behavior may be merely reactive, simply following our natural inclinations. But when we get in the habit of self-reflection, we may realize that our natural inclination may be neither prudent nor charitable. We need to consciously choose the good; virtue is not virtuous if we have no option to do otherwise.

Thus it is by self-reflection that we might become aware, for example, that our inclination to react with equanimity is in some cases the prudent (virtuous) course to take, but in other cases it's not. It will be easier for Luke to develop the virtue of patience, for he is predisposed to it through his temperament. But it may be harder for him to develop the virtue of holy audacity. Yet for Luke to become a man of good and strong character, capable of loving truly, he will need to develop *all* the virtues.[40] A sincere effort to grow in self-knowledge brings us to true humility, without which no real progress in the interpersonal or spiritual life can be made.

Our friends often help us see something in ourselves we might have overlooked. This is why fraternal correction is a work of mercy. Upon humble self-reflection, Luke gradually came to realize how he was succumbing to his natural tendency to let others take charge, to go along with the flow, and to avoid conflict. That deep-seated fear of being alone (at the root of all fear, the Pope says[41]) was coloring his daily interactions with his girlfriend — without his really being aware of it. Indeed, there was virtue in his natural disposition, but it was not true love.

---

[40]We are speaking here about acquired moral virtues, those that one can, through effort, develop (cf. CCC, no. 1839).

[41]Ratzinger, *Introduction to Christianity*.

And Nancy picked up on this as well. She began to wonder whether they were truly right for each other. She had accused Luke of "lacking initiative" and being "indecisive" (a choleric female may act as though she always wants to take charge, but she doesn't want her partner to be a milquetoast!). Nancy's provocative tone was designed to shake Luke out of the doldrums, but he went on as satisfied with the status quo as ever. Finally, Luke went on a spiritual retreat during which he prayed about the relationship, his goals in life, and his relationship with Christ. Eventually, the grace of the retreat and the commitment to growing in self-awareness and in virtue resulted in the couple's breaking up.

> Don't assume a melancholic or a phlegmatic is unhappy, just because he doesn't express wild enthusiasm. Ask him how he feels.

Even though Luke and Nancy (wisely) broke up, don't take this as a sign that couples of diametrically opposed temperaments are doomed to failure. In fact, many couples with opposite temperaments are able to recognize from the start that although their reactions are radically different, their differences complement each other and make them a more well-rounded team. ("If they were all one part, where would the body be?"[42]) These are the couples who laugh at their own foibles and appreciate what the other brings to the table.

The refund

Phlegmatic Joe and choleric Betsy are one such couple. Joe was picking up his choleric wife from the hairdresser when he noticed

[42] 1 Cor. 12:19.

a small sign on the desk. Immediately he hoped his wife hadn't seen it, for it was just the sort of thing to get his wife's choleric juices flowing: "If we do not give you a receipt, your money will be refunded." But to his chagrin, Betsy did see the sign, and immediately pounced on the sales clerk; she demanded a refund, and an argument ensued. All the while, Joe was inching his way toward the door, hoping not to call attention to himself.

Joe and Betsy laugh about their differences, because they understand how their opposite temperaments give rise to radically divergent ways of reacting to situations. The choleric is up for a battle at any moment, while the phlegmatic finds interpersonal conflict excruciatingly painful and something to be avoided at all costs. Yet because they have a basic understanding and appreciation for each other's temperament differences, Joe can admit that he admires the way feisty Betsy sticks up for her rights, and Betsy is able to see how Joe's easygoing nature smooths some of her choleric rough edges. The *respect* that ensues provides a foundation for dealing with temperament conflicts in a positive way.

For indeed, as Joe and Betsy's little scene at the hairdresser's shows, respect doesn't mean that there will be only agreement and never conflict. But it does mean, first, that conflicts will be addressed in a charitable atmosphere, and secondly, that the resolution of conflicts will lead to an increase in understanding and appreciation, and therefore greater respect.

Once, when we were selling our house, Laraine thought Art should have challenged the realtor's low-ball recommendation for the asking price. "You were just agreeing with him! Why are you making his job so easy?" Laraine demanded. But in working through that argument, and years of others like it, choleric Laraine has learned to value Art's gift for diplomacy and his skill at taking problems in indirect ways. Meanwhile phlegmatic Art learned from Laraine that sometimes you can't just "put up with" a situation, and that direct confrontation, however undesirable, is sometimes necessary.

Working it out

A phlegmatic/choleric couple might sometimes disagree over their very different approaches to work and work-related pressure. The phlegmatic would often prefer to avoid unnecessary work, and definitely wants to avoid pressure, while the choleric thrives on both. A choleric on a project gathers steam like a runaway locomotive. His mellow phlegmatic spouse may feel left behind in the dust. When the choleric spouse's search for additional responsibilities in the workplace or community results in more time away from the family, it can cause consternation for the phlegmatic homebody, who longs above all for quiet evenings together as a family.

One choleric/phlegmatic couple we know found themselves arguing over just that temperament difference. Choleric Mario would zoom home after a whirlwind day of work followed by coaching the kids' soccer team. He had barely crossed the threshold when he would demand, "Isn't dinner on the table yet? I've got only fifteen minutes to eat before I take the kids to Youth Group!"

But phlegmatic Jane was still working on the homemade bread! She simply wanted to have the kids at home, eat a family dinner, and pray a family Rosary. That was enough activity for her. Mario found it frustrating that Jane moved so slowly and had so little ambition (compared with him). But instead of discussing his concern, or helping Jane get more organized and efficient, in typical choleric fashion Mario decided to do everything himself: taking the kids to school, chauffeuring them to their sports (he was coaching, anyway), and then lining up evening activities as well. He began making sarcastic comments about Jane's inability to get anything accomplished. Jane's delicate phlegmatic ego suffered, and soon she was feeling even less capable. She began to withdraw her affection and attention from Mario, instead spending her time talking with friends on the phone and eating, to assuage her feelings of inadequacy, guilt, and unexpressed anger toward her husband.

Their situation exemplifies how pursuing an unhealthy "solution" exacerbates the worst aspects of the temperaments: the choleric's brusque belittling of the slower-moving phlegmatic, and the phlegmatic's tendency to silently withdraw. Choleric Mario threw himself into action rather than deal with the interpersonal processing of feelings, and phlegmatic Jane found herself avoiding the intense pressure of Mario's anger and activity — a classic choleric/phlegmatic snafu.

> **INSTEAD OF**
>
> "You sure were a bump on the log all evening!"
>
> **TRY THIS**
>
> "You look tired and worn out. How can I help?"

Mario and Jane needed to take some time to sit down and discuss the problem in a healthy, charitable way. Mario needed to learn about empathy, speaking personally, and using the softened start-up, and Jane needed to learn to address problems directly, instead of avoiding them. Learning to "hit the pause button" instead of firing off an acerbic comment (Mario) or moping (Jane) required self-sacrifice on both their parts. They both had to be very careful not to make generalizations like "You never initiate" or "You are always a bully," which would only invite further disagreement.

Instead of impatiently telling Jane to "get with the program," Mario needed to speak personally and show some empathy instead of blaming (which is quite difficult for the choleric, as we have discussed): "I am worried that we are not working well together. Is there something I am doing that is bothering you?"

This took great humility and patience. And it took great courage for phlegmatic Jane to tell him how his bullying ways discouraged her, and how his sarcasm did not motivate her, but tempted her to withdraw from him. She used the underlying positive (which was very difficult for her while she was in this discouraged mood) to make this point: "I'm grateful for your commitment to the family and for your hard work. But when you get angry or use that sarcastic tone, I get very discouraged, and I feel even *less* capable of accomplishing anything. I just want to avoid you!"

> **INSTEAD OF**
>
> Saying nothing/withdrawing
>
> **TRY THIS**
>
> "I really don't like it when you raise your voice like that; I'd prefer if we could discuss this problem when you're in a calm frame of mind."

Instead of acting wounded and expecting Mario to read her mind, she had to lean into the problem (very tough for phlegmatics): "So, tell me what is bothering you about my behavior." Jane fought back tears as Mario told her how frustrated he was when she failed to initiate or show enthusiasm.

When the hard-charging choleric slows down and takes time to understand his spouse, and the conflict-averse phlegmatic addresses a problem directly instead of avoiding it, things begin to change — not overnight, but gradually. Mario and Jane began making a conscious choice to react outside their temperament dictates, and to practice self-giving. Now that Mario understood how his overbearing ways pushed Jane away, he was able to practice leading with empathy instead of a demand. When Jane saw how Mario sincerely tried to understand, she found that she was more capable of being forthright and initiating.

And finally they listened, *really* listened, to each other. As Pope Benedict XVI points out, we change for the better when we allow the other's thoughts and feelings into our hearts.[43] Change begins in the listening.

[43]Cameron, *Benedictus*.

SANGUINE/MELANCHOLIC
Partying or pondering

As we've seen, when a man and woman of different temperaments marry, trouble can occur when one spouse assumes that
the other is being intentionally oppositional — stubbornly refusing to adjust his behavior — when, in fact, he's simply acting in
accord with his natural temperament. With no other temperament combination is this as evident as with the diametrically
opposed sanguine/melancholic couple.

In chapter 1, we introduced Ron, a quiet, introspective melancholic, and his wife, Stacy, a vivacious, socially active sanguine.
Melancholic Ron would come home from the office longing to relax quietly in the comfort of his home, only to find Stacy (who had
been at home all day with the kids) anxiously waiting to have a
tête-à-tête as soon as he walked in the door. Ron found himself
avoiding Stacy the minute he walked in the door, barricading
himself in the home office, answering his emails.

The melancholic spouse is often completely baffled by the
way the sanguine can seem to forget about important (to him)
details such as being on time, not interrupting, following the
rules, and being serious about serious matters. The sanguine is be-
mused by the melancholic's chronic pessimism, inflexibility, his
obsessing on things being just so, and his worry-wart nature. Opposites may attract, but sometimes the sanguine and melancholic
seem so totally opposed that you wonder how they make a marriage work!

For Ron and Stacy, the key to working it out involved coming
to understand and accept their temperamental differences, and
then *making small, specific* changes that showed respect for these
differences. Ron saw that Stacy's need for social interaction and

conversation was as deep as his own need for peace and quiet, and he was willing to compromise so that they could both have their core needs met. They settled on a certain number of social events that Stacy would attend (some as a couple, some individually) and they set aside quiet time for Ron.

Stacy resolved to forbear pouncing on Ron as soon as he walked in the door, and instead would give him a few minutes to get acclimated to the home environment. When Ron felt refreshed instead of badgered and harried, he had more mental energy to devote to his wife.

This was important, because he had become so withdrawn that Stacy had begun to feel as if she was in an emotional vacuum. She had a core need to engage Ron in intimate discussions on a regular basis, and it wasn't being met. She also felt that it wasn't "right" for Ron to be so socially reclusive, and so she'd been nagging him to attend social events with her. When he refused, she went by herself, which only increased the emotional distance between them.

> Your spouse will argue with you less if you express your feelings *directly.*

When they both agreed to compromise, scheduling time for Ron to have peace and seclusion, and time for the two of them to talk and go out together, they both became much more relaxed and willing to compromise even more. True, it was initially somewhat difficult for Stacy to understand why she had to *schedule* time to talk; this was something she felt should just "happen" when two people are in love. But once she realized that scheduling the time would actually accomplish her desires, she was willing to go along with it even though it went against her spontaneous sanguine nature.

The law of reciprocal action
Saying that Ron and Stacy "compromised" sounds like a simple, even superficial, solution. Yet it embodies a deep psychological truth. Stacy discovered that cutting back on her own whirlwind of social engagements and volunteer activities mysteriously resulted in Ron's becoming *more* interested in attending (a reasonable number of) social events with her. Having a willing Ron along for the ride for a few parties was far more gratifying than attending many more of them with Ron sulking at home! As Ron attended one or two social events with Stacy, she stopped pestering him constantly about his "antisocial" behavior. When Stacy made the small but significant change of waiting for Ron to decompress after work, she found he was more available to talk.

Newton's third law of motion, "to every action there is an equal and opposite reaction," applies to our marriages too — especially to those marriages of opposite temperaments. If we feel that our spouse is behaving in an extreme fashion (say, too outgoing and sociable or too isolated and withdrawn), we will be strongly tempted to compensate with the opposite extreme behavior — thereby ensuring that neither of us is acting in a balanced way at all! Melancholic Ron said, "She *always* wants to go out, so I *always* have to say no!" And Stacy complained, "Ron never wants to talk, so I have to badger him constantly about what is going on in his life!"

Sanguine/melancholic couples are particularly prone to the "unbalanced balancing act," simply because their temperaments exemplify the extremes. A sanguine dad finds himself overly permissive with his kids, because he feels his wife is too strict a disciplinarian. For her part, she doesn't like being cast in the role of "the heavy," but she feels she *has* to, or nobody will do it. There is the sanguine mom who is over-involved in her parish and her children's school, while her husband is never seen. She feels she *has* to volunteer for everything, because her melancholic husband says no to everything. While such behaviors lend the illusion of "balancing" the marriage, these reactive postures actually end up polarizing the spouses.

We can now see how the resolution that had initially seemed almost clichéd — compromise — is not only psychologically sound, but virtuous. For virtue can be defined as a mean between excess and defect; as a couple, Ron and Stacy learned to practice the golden mean between opposite temperaments. In so doing, Ron grew in sociability and solidarity, and Stacy in patience and temperance.

You say tomato, and I say tomahto

Sanguine Kyle and melancholic Lydia were very different temperamentally, but shared core values: their Catholic faith and their commitment to raising their children with strong morals. During their sixteen years of marriage, they always had worked through their differences, although they each had a radically different approach. Kyle was happily impulsive, while Lydia carefully attended to details before taking a step forward.

"You're so pessimistic," Kyle would complain, while Lydia calmly insisted that she was *realistic,* not pessimistic. She was looking at the actual *facts,* while Kyle preferred to see rosy fantasy. Kyle was a high school teacher, a job he found so rewarding that he typically came home from work in a good mood, filled with hearty cheer. Lydia spent her day keeping the home in perfect order and attending to all the minutiae of their schedules — kids' activities and homework, doctor appointments — and her own part-time job as a bookkeeper.

Their radically different approaches to problem-solving came to a head when their oldest child entered an academically demanding high school and got off to a typically phlegmatic slow start. He was no longer an "A" student; he was spending a lot of time in sports activities rather than studies, and his room was a complete disaster. He often forgot assignments and procrastinated on projects. His teachers were sending home notes of concern.

"He'll get the hang of it!" declared Kyle optimistically. Being a high school teacher himself, he knew it was tough for many kids their first semester. Kyle and his son headed to the gym to lift weights. They came back sweaty and happy, only to meet the full force of Lydia's anger. "I don't see how you can take this so lightly! He's barely passing in math, and every stitch of clothing he owns is on the floor of his room! He doesn't have time to do his chores anymore, because he has so much homework. Then you both go off to the gym as though nothing was wrong!"

Lydia's frustration grew in direct proportion to Kyle's soft-pedaling. While Kyle breezily dismissed Lydia's concerns in his sanguine fashion, Lydia grew hyperconscious of the details. She checked her son's room, made lists of household chores he was neglecting, scrutinized his planner, and sent emails to his teachers to make sure he was turning in his homework. She even periodically opened his cell phone to see how many calls he was making, and at what time. If he placed a call after 10 p.m., she objected.

Melancholic Lydia believed that their son was endangering his future. Sanguine Kyle thought Lydia was obsessively overreacting to a first-quarter slump — that kids should enjoy being kids while they can, and learn from their own mistakes.

Because they are at the opposite ends of the temperament spectrum, sanguine/melancholic couples often face just this sort of quandary: the sanguine wants to be flexible, look on the bright side, and make generous allowances for socializing, while the melancholic focuses attention on the critical details, fearful that the truly important things of life will be overtaken by frivolities. Kyle and Lydia were caught in a classic vicious circle: the sanguine feeling he must be more tolerant and optimistic, because the melancholic was too critical; the melancholic thinking she had to crack down, because the sanguine wasn't taking things seriously enough.

Kyle and Lydia needed to remind themselves that they *both* loved their children and wanted them to achieve success. They had the same goal! Yet each one reacted out of fear that the other's behavior was jeopardizing its success. After affirming to each other that they were on the same team, they were brought to see how they'd been "typecasting" each other with broad generalizations: saying (and thinking) things like, "You never discipline the kids!" or "You always think the worst about every situation!" Such comments became self-fulfilling when each overreacted to counter the other's perceived failings. *Only* when they consciously fought the tendency to typecast were they able to rein in their own temperamental excesses.

> Melancholics and phlegmatics need time to think things over. A forced, quick response tends not to be an honest one.

Guess what happened? The vicious circle reversed itself: Kyle and Lydia stopped seeing themselves as "oppositional," always needing to cancel out the other with ever-more-extreme temperamental behaviors, and instead grew more united in their approach. They were able to re-focus on their shared goals. Most important, they stopped trying to change each other and instead worked on changing themselves: Kyle agreed to address the low grades with their son, and Lydia relaxed her vigilant monitoring.

Together they worked on a plan to help their son balance his school and extracurricular activities. No longer quarreling about who was too lenient and who was a taskmaster, sanguine husband and melancholic wife were able once again to respect each other.

Chapter 8

∞

Kindred Spirits

"Like kindred drops,
been mingled into one."
William Cowper

∞

We have looked at couples whose temperaments were completely opposite: the choleric/phlegmatic and the melancholic/sanguine. In this chapter, we will look at those couples who have temperaments that share some, but not all features; they're similar in some respects, yet dissimilar in others. The result of such pairings is often that a particular tendency is heightened, because they will have areas in which they both tend to react in just the same way.

For example, the choleric/sanguine couple is an outgoing, action-oriented, somewhat impatient team. The phlegmatic/melancholic combination (both being introverts) will tend to be more subdued, with an emphasis on the interior life. The choleric/melancholic couple is strong on being right and being in control, while the sanguine/phlegmatic couple is mellow and flexible.

In the following sections, we outline a few areas in which these couples are most likely to excel, and also those areas in which they might collide. Remember, learning to work through the "collisions" makes us grow in virtue. As Pope Benedict XVI wrote (as Cardinal Ratzinger): "Fulfillment does not lie in ... following one's inclinations, but precisely in allowing demands to be made upon you, in taking the harder path."[44] Although following our natural temperament inclination might be the easier path, it is not as rewarding as growing in virtue and learning new ways to support our spouse and express our love.

[44]Cardinal Joseph Ratzinger, *God and the World: A Conversation with Peter Seewald* (San Francisco: Ignatius Press, 2002).

The Temperament God Gave Your Spouse

MELANCHOLIC/CHOLERIC
Taking the "A" train

In 1944, a young Foreign Service officer was temporarily assigned to the State Department, while waiting for paperwork he needed to join the Navy. Choleric Emma was working in that office and noticed the very handsome gentleman. When all her attempts to draw his attention were to no avail, she perched flirtatiously atop his desk and chattered at length about a new movie in town. She was hoping he'd take the hint and ask her out. Instead, melancholic Jerome pronounced seriously, "Well, I certainly should see that movie," and went back to work. After his paperwork came through, he left the office and Emma thought she would never see him again. But several weeks later, she received a letter from him asking her to go out to dinner. Four months later, they were married! The marriage might not have happened were it not for the natural assertiveness of the choleric.

Emma was decisive and outgoing, while Jerome was more cautious and reserved, yet their marriage lasted forty-four happy years. But let's take a look at another melancholic/choleric couple, for whom trouble ensued over their shared tendency to *control*.

Ingrid is what we call a turbo-charged melancholic: an intense, serious perfectionist. Her home is perfect (her motto is, "Your home should be ready to go on the market at any given moment"), thanks to her meticulous care. She's even been known to climb on the roof after a big storm to inspect the shingles! Her husband, Richard, is equally determined (and opinionated), but his more extraverted, less introspective nature labels him a choleric. Together, they make quite an intimidating couple.

Their children, when young, were silent and respectful. Ingrid had trained them to play in the basement with their friends, so they wouldn't mess up the main living area. And they weren't off the hook for cleaning up the basement after playtime. Where a sanguine would have shrugged, "That's what basements are for" (and probably joined in the fun), Ingrid saw to it that *every* nook and cranny of her house remained immaculate. Ingrid and Richard's children made sure the neighborhood playmates got the message, too, and nobody was allowed to go home until the basement had been tidied. The net result was (to Ingrid and Richard) what counted: an orderly home and obedient offspring.

Everything about their family life was planned,

> When a melancholic makes a critical comment, it doesn't mean he's unhappy or angry. (But melancholics must realize that most people don't understand this!)

including which college the kids would attend (decided when they were born, and the college fund created); where to live (with the best school district); and which Sunday Mass would be attended. Ingrid was on the PTA board, and Richard kept moving up the corporate ladder.

Some chinks in the family armor appeared when the children hit adolescence, and both became equally stubborn and opinionated, although (mirroring their parents) each manifested this in a different way: one became silently stubborn, and the other became overtly so. The children had inherited their parents' strong will and sharp intellect. Adolescence is a time of awakening individuality and serious questioning — especially for the choleric adolescent. Ingrid and Richard's children, true to both temperament and developmental stage, began to demand compelling arguments for their parents' rules and regulations. Neither compliant phlegmatics nor people-pleasing sanguines, their children even dared to disagree!

The melancholic/choleric couple was used to being in charge and having everything under control. When children are small, this is not so difficult, and with motivated parents, a household can indeed be made to run like a tight ship. At times, Richard and Ingrid were not only "in control" of their family; they were also *controlling*. They had grown used to everyone following their orders. They hadn't realized that their rather authoritarian "because I said so" approach to parenting might induce in their choleric adolescents an urgent need to ask "why?" and even to dissent.

It is true of any adolescent, but especially of cholerics: when the kids grow into teens, parents can no longer rely on simple commands to keep the ship afloat. The task of parenting shifts from *control* to *influence*. When Ingrid and Richard tried to cling to their old ways of control, their previously calm home turned into a battle zone. They fought for control of the children — as Chess and Thomas put it, "constantly shaping their child's behavior to suit their own convenience and preferences."[45] They fought about who was right, and when the children couldn't be controlled, who was wrong. At times they stopped speaking, each convinced that the other was at fault. Ingrid and Richard were nearly at the end of their rope when they finally turned to counseling.

Being in control, but not controlling

Both melancholics and cholerics can be very strong-willed and thus want to take control — the choleric openly so, the melancholic behind the scenes or even passive-aggressively. If the two spouses disagree on parenting, battle lines may be drawn and

[45]Chess and Thomas, *Temperament in Clinical Practice.*

prisoners taken! The pragmatic choleric spouse may be more willing to bend the rules in order to make things work — a tactic that offends the idealistic melancholic. In turn, the choleric may react angrily when the melancholic is very critical or overly obsessed with the rules. This can hurt the more sensitive melancholic's feelings. Both temperaments can be prone to unforgiveness and holding on to hurts or transgressions.

In the process of seeking help for their children, Richard and Ingrid had to face up to these tendencies, and in so doing, they also learned something about their own approach to life and to their marriage. They had been operating in separate spheres of influence for many years (Ingrid managing the home and Richard in the workforce) until the behavior of the preteen and teenager forced Richard to intervene. When choleric Richard took charge too forcefully, his family felt pushed around and pushed aside. As a boss, Richard was used to receiving respect and seeing prompt action, and he expected this attitude to prevail at home as well. When the family "failed" on this count, Richard became angry and resentful. Meanwhile, melancholic Ingrid vented her frustrations by working even harder in her home and making even more rigorous demands on the kids.

Ingrid's rigor spilled over to the way she treated Richard, too, and she began to criticize him moralistically. Richard then felt she was being disloyal and undermining his authority as father and head of the household. Ingrid's response to this was usually to seethe

> **INSTEAD OF**
>
> "A good father would know how important it is to have a family dinner!"
>
> **TRY THIS**
>
> "I know how much pressure you're under with the new boss, but I would really love to schedule a family night, at least once a week."

quietly or (even worse) to revisit past hurts and transgressions, filling the atmosphere of the home with constant unresolved tension and anger. Both spouses strongly believed that they were right; neither wanted to give way.

Learning new skills

When the kids were young and controllable, and things seemed to be going smoothly, Richard and Ingrid had never felt the need to examine their communication patterns, but now they were forced to face their temperamental tendencies and make changes for the better — before their stubborn natures allowed the marriage to be harmed beyond the point of repair.

First, choleric Richard had to learn to be more *empathic* than he is naturally inclined. This is important for any choleric who wants a happy marriage, but especially so when he's married to a sensitive melancholic. The need is amplified further when his spouse is also partially phlegmatic, and therefore not well-equipped to handle the choleric's brusque and straightforward communication style. Here the choleric must once again turn to the *softened start-up*, training himself to develop the empathy needed to appreciate how his spouse will perceive what he says (and not just the way he thinks his spouse "should" perceive it!).

Melancholic Ingrid had to learn to tone down her criticism, mentally vowing to make five positive comments for every negative one. The choleric spouse is an achiever who focuses on the bottom line and doesn't take well to seeing his hard work or big plans torn down by (to him) nitpicking criticism. Sometimes it's also difficult for cholerics to allow others to have influence over them, for this reveals vulnerability. Ingrid had to learn to assert herself in the marital partnership in ways that didn't trigger the choleric's defense mechanisms — and the arguments that inevitably ensued.

Eventually, both spouses needed to grow in empathy toward their children, to recognize that as teens they didn't respond the way they did when they were younger, and to learn to relax a little in their management of the household. Ingrid needed to ease up on her tight controls over the children, and to grow in the virtue (it is hard for melancholics to believe it is a virtue) of flexibility. Richard needed to learn how to take charge without alienating everyone else.

INSTEAD OF	TRY THIS
"That's ridiculous!"	"Tell me more about your idea."

Both needed to recognize that their children's questions alone did not imply insubordination or disrespect, and that if they'd only be open to dialogue, some fruitful discussions might result. (This didn't mean the parents had to agree with their kids — only that they were willing to talk. Refusing to engage in dialogue at all often sends the undesirable message to their teens that their parents' position cannot be *reasonably* defended.)

One small but effective change they made was simply to create a family night and allowing their children to choose the activities *they* wanted (even if Ingrid was tempted to think them unserious or Richard to think them unproductive). The kids felt the reins loosen, the spouses got a break from the stress of planning and working, and everyone began to enjoy each other's company and to reconnect in a positive way. Ingrid and Richard spoke more openly with each other and with the children about their hopes and dreams for the family. They allowed the children more freedom to express ideas or complaints.

Later the couple took up the daily practice of *forgiving* each other for real or perceived transgressions, never letting the sun set on their anger,[46] and the more loving attitude that resulted also helped the children immensely. They could never have seen it before, but the couple realized that their affection for each other, creating an atmosphere of understanding, acceptance, and respect, helped their children even more than their exacting standards and stringent rules had.

[46]Eph. 4:26.

CHOLERIC/SANGUINE
Look out, world!

She's an intelligent, strong-willed, ambitious lawyer. He's a successful politician, with a down-home style that charms the ladies. She is choleric, he is sanguine. A match made in (political) heaven? You guessed it: Bill and Hillary Clinton.

You know the criticisms, too. Hillary is said to be opportunistic, always wanting to have her way, and rolling over people who oppose it. Bill is considered to be less principled morally, overly spontaneous, and indiscreet. A friend of ours told us that one time he was caddying for President Clinton, who apparently had no qualms about asking his opinion about an upcoming political statement he was planning to make. Clinton is known for being quick to apologize when he has made a mistake, and wanting to forget about it and move on — just like a sanguine!

A choleric/sanguine match will allow many opportunities to take on interesting and challenging adventures. Both temperaments want to be actively involved out in the world, but each will have a slightly different emphasis: the sanguine will notice the people, wanting to build relationships, while the choleric will keep a sharp eye out for the opportunities, desiring to achieve goals. Choleric ambition partnered with sanguine generosity creates a dynamic team, especially when the Faith provides the necessary grounding to their highly active natures. The sanguine has a tendency to bite off more than he can chew (thanks to his superb salesmanship), but the choleric can help him prioritize his tasks and persevere to the end. Cholerics, meanwhile, can sometimes be accused of looking past people (and their feelings) in focusing on the goal, but the sanguine can show him how to be happy smelling all the roses along the way.

And so, although both are extraverts, they will have a complementary focus that's mutually beneficial. The sanguine can teach his choleric spouse forgiveness and flexibility, and help the choleric to remember that people are ultimately more important than achievements; that empathy and sensitivity in our human relationships will help us draw closer to one another and to the Lord. Meanwhile, the choleric can help his sanguine spouse retain a bit more focus and clarity about his goals. Most sanguines can use a dose of choleric perseverance, as well as the intensity of concentration that a choleric always seems to have in abundance!

Both temperaments can work on listening and developing interpersonal depth: the choleric because he tends to fear too much self-disclosure, and the sanguine through a tendency to lack introspection. Thus, the two will need to allow for time spent in getting to know each other in depth — through evenings spent talking, just the two of them, and through structured spiritual opportunities, such as marriage-enrichment events. Otherwise, the tendency might be to have a little too much action and not enough reflection.

Living large

Thanks to their outgoing natures, the choleric's aspirations to greatness, and the sanguine's conviviality, their family will be expansive, energetic, and life-loving as well. One choleric/sanguine couple we know has seven highly active kids. Even if they all hadn't been active by nature, they soon learned to be so from their environment. Their house is loud and in constant flux. Children fly in like dervishes from sports and after-school activities, tossing cleats and lacrosse sticks in the entry hall, before heading out for more activities. Mom is whipping up a gourmet meal in the kitchen while chatting into her Bluetooth with her dinner guests.

The children are not only highly accomplished athletes, but also are well-read and musically talented. The parents encourage bold adventure, risk-taking, and even pranks! An unsuspecting guest has been known to trip the cup of water rigged above the doorway, finding himself drenched to the sound of muffled guffaws. It's not all fun and games, either, because this couple has high aspirations for the family: exotic vacations, high-profile ventures, and Ivy League colleges are on the agenda.

The sanguine/choleric couple will have big dreams and will likely have many great successes in life. The family described above is not only successful in the natural sphere but also is well-formed in their faith and dedicated to serving the Church. Without such a strong commitment to the Faith, such a couple would have to guard against becoming overly immersed in the vanity of the world and the allure of money, power, or fame. With faith as their sure foundation, they are leaders for Christ.

They say the neon lights are bright . . . on Broadway

Indeed, the foundation of the Faith is necessary for all temperaments, but especially for the extraverted choleric and sanguine. These temperaments tend to be so adept on the natural level that they can be dismissive of the interior and spiritual realms. Without sufficient self-reflection, they may lose their moral and spiritual compass. They may be successful, but on a superficial and worldly level only. They are enthusiastic and motivated . . . but for the *right* things?

The impulsivity of the sanguine also might result in emotions running high, with the choleric becoming annoyed by his spouse's volatility. He may then respond in anger, and an argument may ensue. A sanguine female, with her natural attraction to fashion, glitz, and flamboyance, might attract more attention than her husband is comfortable with. He might assume she is flirting. The choleric might try to control (in a domineering way) the flighty sanguine, who will resent such control and feel hurt by it.

Still, not all volatility (a hallmark of the choleric/sanguine marriage) is destructive. Although you may think that argumentative couples are likely to be doomed, this is not necessarily the case, according to the research. Gottman discovered that those couples who had big blow-ups could have long and happy marriages — provided their arguments took place within the context of a warm, loving relationship. In fact, the volatile couples tended to express not only their disagreements; they were also very expressive of affection, humor, joy, and passion.

> Don't assume a choleric is angry with you, if he is merely arguing a point.

Still, a sanguine/choleric couple can be so impulsive that they can make poor choices for their family. For example, one highly successful sanguine/choleric couple abruptly pulled all their children out of their Catholic school in the middle of the year. Their oldest child had been put on academic probation. They felt he should be given special treatment, because he was such a talented athlete and they were a prominent family. The administration didn't budge, and they withdrew all their kids in a huff and put them in the local public school.

But the biggest problem facing such a couple is their tendency to activism. Without the benefit of an introspective spouse to ground them, cholerics and sanguines often throw themselves into activities and work — even good and noble projects — without taking the time to discern (through prayer and reflection) whether such activity is God's will for them. This can affect their children, their faith, and ultimately their marriage.

First and foremost, a sanguine/choleric couple needs to practice discerning their decisions in light of the Lord's will. This will take self-control for the autocratic choleric and the impetuous sanguine. It's difficult for all of us to submit our will to another authority, but most of all for the choleric — even when that authority is the highest.

On the natural level, the sanguine/choleric couple can practice some of those communication skills that are particularly helpful when the subject is delicate and emotions are running high: particularly the softened start-up and empathic listening. Together, they will need to work on being open to each other's influence; else they will be quite likely to spin off in their own separate directions.

> **INSTEAD OF**
>
> "We never go on vacation! All you do is work, work, work!"
>
> **TRY THIS**
>
> "It's been two years since we went away for our vacation. Let's work on a budget, and see if we can swing it this year!"

The Temperament God Gave Your Spouse

SANGUINE/PHLEGMATIC
Happy meets harmony

This will be an easygoing match, especially if the sanguine is part phlegmatic! Both love harmony and fun, and want to please each other. The fun-loving and interactive sanguine will help the introverted phlegmatic come out of his shell, as well as provide the enthusiasm that a phlegmatic needs to get motivated. Meanwhile, the phlegmatic will provide a helpful (and instructive) counter-balance to the sanguine's impulsiveness.

Neither the happy-go-lucky sanguine nor the contented phlegmatic will be overly demanding of the other, unless the sanguine is also partly choleric. If the two are both laid-back and accepting of life and of each other, they will need to watch out for becoming *too* accommodating, lest career opportunities go unpursued, household repairs wait for years, or real needs for self-improvement are ignored. The sanguine's short attention span, combined with the phlegmatic's tendency to procrastinate, can lead to piles of unpaid bills, library fines, video-store late fees, and last-minute requests for tax-filing extensions.

Fortunately, though, the kind of motivation phlegmatics need — positive and involved — is just the kind a sanguine excels at providing. Meanwhile, the solid but never showy phlegmatic grounds the flighty sanguine.

For both temperaments, high-pressure nagging tends to have the opposite of the desired effect: the phlegmatic withdraws in discomfort, while the sanguine is liable to have his feelings hurt. The phlegmatic spouse should remember that the affectionate sanguine craves attention, romance, and adventure; he might have to make an extra effort to remember important dates such as anniversaries, birthdays, and other important milestones, and to recognize them — even if he himself can't understand what all the fuss is about.

One sanguine/phlegmatic couple we know has a relationship that's almost frivolously (as viewed by a choleric or melancholic!) light and happy. They enjoy watching the latest movies, going to baseball games, and just hanging out at home. Neither needs to shop at the most expensive stores, they aren't looking to keep up with the Joneses, and they're content with low-key activities and socializing with a small group of friends. They both tend to forget important details ("Where did we put the checkbook, honey?"), to procrastinate, and they definitely lack "ambition" in the classic sense of the term. But they are unpretentious homebodies who love children and have the patience of Job and the willingness to work hard and long hours — so long as they can see light at the end of the tunnel. After struggling through taxes or bill-paying, they will head out for an ice-cream cone. After long hours at work, they will happily snuggle on the couch, watching television. They love to go everywhere together — movies, ball games and Mass, and their strength as a couple improves dramatically when they work together on their spiritual life.

When emotions run high

Not everything is always peaceful in sanguine/phlegmatic world, though. If the sociable sanguine gets overextended in personal commitments, he can become overwrought, and this will stress out the phlegmatic, who likes serenity and routine (which the sanguine may come to find a little boring). Plus, the extraverted sanguine's response to stress is quite distinct from the introverted phlegmatic's.

Sanguine Janine loved the fact that phlegmatic Aaron was so quietly dependable and trustworthy, with such integrity. Aaron found Janine fun, exciting, and energizing. Things always seemed to be popping when Janine was around. They married (*she* proposed), and everything was going smoothly until the first baby came. Janine's emotions ran amok with lack of sleep. She had always talked a lot as a way of sorting out her problems, but now the talking seemed incessant. Aaron was working harder (feeling the responsibility to provide for a new baby) and wasn't home as early as he used to be. He came home tired, just wanting to relax on the couch, but Janine handed him a squalling baby as soon as he walked through the door.

Janine was anxious about her new role as mom, missed the adult conversations she used to have at work, and needed help around the house, especially in the evenings, when the baby was cranky and she was trying to get dinner on the table. And she couldn't seem to refrain from airing every (usually negative) thought at every moment! Overwhelmed by all the complaining, Aaron began tuning Janine out, which only hurt her feelings and shifted her complaining into overdrive: "You *never* do anything around the house!" and "Do I have to raise this baby alone?!" Easygoing Aaron was finding the home atmosphere so unbearable that he contemplated leaving the house.

We remember bringing our first child home from the hospital; an impossibly tiny person, entirely our responsibility, slumped in the enormous car seat. (Why had they permitted us to leave the hospital? Couldn't they see how ill-equipped we were for this monumental job?) For every new parent, there is an often-difficult period of adjustment that can be made harder by hormones, tight spaces, and lack of sleep. For Janine and Aaron, the adjustment was also intensified by their particular temperaments. Aaron's calm approach usually had a steadying effect on Janine, but now his understated response to her exaggerated emotions seemed heartless. "How can he be so laid-back? Doesn't he *understand* how upset I am? Doesn't he *care?*" Janine wanted action, and she wanted it *now.*

Fortunately, Aaron had a flash of insight (or maybe it was the Holy Spirit; phlegmatics seldom have "flashes" of any kind) and bought a plane ticket for Janine's mom to come visit a month earlier than she had planned to. It was worth the investment. Janine's mom had an immediate calming effect on the household. She was there to talk with Janine during the day, to lend her experience, to help out at the difficult dinner hour. And, with her mom there to watch the baby, the couple could even get out on occasion for a walk around the neighborhood, when they were able to have some heart-to-heart talks.

When we are under stress (a new baby, a new job, a move), our preferred styles of interacting might fall short and, indeed, might even cause more trouble. Sanguine Janine reacted to stress by talking more, expressing her negative feelings in a shrill, almost hysterical manner. Aaron reacted to stress by working harder (at work), then coming home even quieter and more withdrawn than usual. His low-key reaction to Janine's emotionality (theretofore quite welcome) now only fueled Janine's fire.

Now Aaron and Janine learned that they needed to make a conscious decision to change tactics in certain situations. Phlegmatic Aaron realized that discussing problems could have more of a calming effect on Janine than merely absorbing them, and

> **INSTEAD OF**
>
> Saying nothing/ignoring a problem
>
> **TRY THIS**
>
> "I realize our house isn't in prime shape after all these years and kids. Let's sit down together and maybe we can come up with a plan for getting started on fixing things up."

Janine realized that she needed to bring up her needs less impulsively, with more sensitivity, so that she was expressing herself in a more positive, charitable manner. She needed to speak more personally and specifically about how she felt, rather than blaming Aaron. (Saying, "I'm feeling anxious about whether I'll be a good mother," rather than "You never help me with the baby!")

Janine's new way of expressing herself helped Aaron understand what was really bothering her. They both had pent-up hurt feelings, which only a little empathy could soothe. In this atmosphere of mutual understanding and self-sacrifice, Janine and Aaron worked through a tough, but rewarding, time of their young married life.

PHLEGMATIC/MELANCHOLIC
Steady as they go

A melancholic/phlegmatic couple can make a quiet, steady, and faithful team that provides a deep and solid foundation for their family. The phlegmatic will steady the anxious melancholic, while the melancholic supplies the prone-to-complacency phlegmatic with a noble sense of purpose. Since the phlegmatic partner does not usually show the same intensity or depth as the melancholic, his rather prosaic approach to life can test his melancholic spouse's patience at times. But what the phlegmatic might lack in terms of profundity, he makes up for with his unpretentious service.

The phlegmatic's quietly supportive ways of providing for the family, maintaining the home, or helping with the kids can easily go unnoticed. The melancholic should take care to acknowledge the phlegmatic's unfailing good nature — in fact, be grateful for it. No other temperament is as well-equipped to put up with the typical melancholic's high standards and heavy demands! Plus, the typical phlegmatic dry wit brings lightness to melancholic gloom.

The ugly fridge
Father Joseph Massman comments that the melancholic's deep feelings for the ideals of virtue, order, and beauty are easily wounded when confronted with defects and sin, which may result in "bitterness and vexation of spirit."[47] He begins to brood and find fault in himself and in others. But a melancholic longs for truth, and when he humbly seeks it, he can find his way out of discouragement and frustration.

[47] Joseph Massman, *Nervousness, Temperament, and the Soul* (Fort Collins: Roman Catholic Books, 1941).

Our melancholic friend Mary Beth did just that. She and her phlegmatic husband, Ed, are both extremely intelligent and dedicated at home and on the job, and attentive to their five children. Ed is laid-back, soft-spoken, and although he quietly goes about his work, he'd rather be a gentleman farmer — a prospect melancholic Mary Beth finds less than enticing. But she indulgently lets him buy cows, chickens, and even hogs.

Our daughters were in a girls' club together, and we needed a location for the annual end-of-year party. We expected fifty girls and their moms to attend, and we planned to have a bonfire and roast marshmallows and hot dogs. We needed space for the games, skits, and awards, and Mary Beth's home was perfect: several acres with a pool, a barn, and those farm animals.

Melancholic Mary Beth said yes, but then vacillated. What if it rained and soaked the wood for the bonfire, and all those people wanted to come inside? Could one bathroom accommodate fifty girls? What if someone got too close to the bonfire and was burned? What if one of the girls impaled herself on a sharp stick we were using for skewers? What if (horror) one of the other moms happened to see the old, rusted refrigerator in the basement?

We told M. B. that we would pray for good weather and would warn the girls about the skewers, and reminded her that she herself was on hand as a pediatric nurse. In addition, the girls would help clean the house before and after the party.

But there was no fixing that fridge.

The day before the party, Mary Beth decided to paint the appalling fridge. This took a lot more time than she had anticipated, and during the process, she lectured herself: "Is it pride or vanity that is making me jump through hoops just for a bunch of girls? Why do I care what the fridge looks like? Will anyone notice, anyway? Ed loves this old fridge!"

Halfway through, Mary Beth realized that it was not a wise use of her time, that a little dose of humility couldn't hurt, and so instead, she painted on the fridge a little love message to her husband.

The party was a huge success. The weather was sunny and warm. No injuries occurred. Moreover, nobody noticed the rusty parts of the fridge or the dated Harvest Gold color. What caught people's attention was, "I love you, Ed!" painted in big, bold letters across the front.

Melancholics are the most self-reflective of all the temperaments. Our friend Mary Beth utilized this temperament strength to overcome a temperament weakness (being overly critical). She challenged herself to be humble and loving (counteracting both pride and vanity), and transformed a household eyesore into a banner of appreciation for her husband.

Near occasions of nagging

We've seen before, though, that too much nitpicking can darken the spirits of the phlegmatic and cause him to withdraw, and unfortunately, if it's nitpicking you're looking for, you'll usually find it from a melancholic! But one way for a melancholic to avoid "near occasions of nagging" is to stay occupied. Although melancholics can appear to require a lot of down time (since they require solitude to recharge), in reality *too much* unstructured time contributes to fussing, nitpicking, and behind-the-scenes controlling of everyone else's lives! The under-utilized melancholic will turn his perfectionist attention to dwell upon ways in which the phlegmatic falls short — in conversation, in personal appearance, and in the romance department.

But that doesn't mean the phlegmatic has nothing to learn from his melancholic spouse. One phlegmatic we know, married for more than half a century to an exacting, artistic melancholic, has encountered a world through her that he never would have found on his own. Although he rarely ventures beyond the daily newspaper and the cowboy tales of Louis L'Amour, his wife reads snippets aloud from her vast library: theology, literature, philosophy, history, and poetry. She takes him along to art galleries and museums, to the opera, and to concerts to broaden his horizons. His heart swells with pride when he invites guests to their home, beautifully decorated and pristinely organized far beyond his ken. He says he can't imagine life without his wife's artistic sensibility and high tastes.

Solid, if not scintillating

Melancholic and phlegmatic spouses are likely to be very committed to their faith, and focused on morals and building character in their children. However, they will not typically be guilty of overactivism. If they are involved in their parish, it may be in a more understated capacity, such as the Altar Society or the Prayer Tree. (Leave it to the sanguine/choleric couple to head up fundraising or the parish Casino Night.)

Likewise, they make solid and reliable parents, but not usually exciting ones. They'll want to watch out, therefore, that the tone of the household doesn't become overly somber and quiet — especially if there are sanguine children! This quiet temperament combination probably rarely throw a party or go on an adventure, but their children (especially when they're teens) will want to have some fun, at least every once in a while. Just as a choleric/melancholic couple can drive teenagers to rebellion with too-high standards enforced in a controlling way, the phlegmatic/melancholic couple can invite rebellion by being unrelentingly humdrum.

It is often a melancholic/phlegmatic couple who will undertake the noble venture of homeschooling. This temperament combination will likely have the determination necessary to persevere, yet the couple should be on guard against creating an insular environment that insufficiently challenges and motivates their children, or a fortress mentality that disdains the positive influences of (as well as the potential to evangelize) the culture. And if the melancholic/phlegmatic couple is too quiet, too critical, and lacking in the warmth and vibrancy that extraverted parents provide, the children may wind up trying to draw their parents' attention with annoying, bickering, troublemaking behaviors. If the household becomes one where overt positive attention is rarely given, children may find they prefer negative attention to a depressing or self-critical mood.

> It takes self-control to use the softened start-up, when I really want to blurt out all my anger and my pent-up feelings.

The low-key aspect of a phlegmatic/melancholic couple can sometimes give rise to an overall lack of initiative in the household, followed closely (especially if the melancholic is secondarily choleric) by a critical/complaining (rather than a can-do) tone. One melancholic/phlegmatic couple we know was flummoxed by a particularly intractable teen. Both parents were hard-working and dutiful, and not given to motivating discussions around the dinner table. After one halfhearted attempt to garner his preferred job at a bookstore, their son declared himself unable to find *any-thing*. To his parents' dismay, thereafter he slept in every morning and hung out with his gainfully employed friends at night.

His parents didn't realize that they would need to take action (*action* is *not* the operative word in a phlegmatic/melancholic match) in order to motivate the boy. Mom complained to Dad, who avoided addressing the issue, thinking that eventually the boy would become inspired. Neither parent was inclined to become personally involved in the matter, for they both believed that it was their son's responsibility to find his own work. They had forgotten, however, that their own work ethic had been forged over many years of adulthood; in fact, when they were young, they'd needed family connections to help them find their first jobs. Unable to see that intervention was called for, the quietly plodding couple had left their young teen with neither example nor inspiration from which to draw, to take that first scary leap into the world.

Love in the key of mellow

The subdued phlegmatic/melancholic couple will also tend to be more reserved in expressing affection. This couple may have been uncharacteristically demonstrative — even passionate — during their courtship, but once they settle into a daily routine (and once their family starts growing), they will often revert to their more comfortable, introverted ways. The failure to extend to one another the emotional warmth they each need, the tendency to forget to express overt praise and appreciation may not seem problematic at first, but over the decades, small blisters can become a serious wound.

> **INSTEAD OF**
>
> "You're so insensitive!"
>
> **TRY THIS**
>
> "I really could use a hug right now. I'm feeling down."

The melancholic may sometimes seem too high-minded to care about silly things like little gestures of tenderness and appreciation; the phlegmatic's outward mask may not seem to be affected, no matter what you say or don't say to him, but time and

again, research shows that happily married couples of *any* temperament combination are ones who express an abundance of positive sentiments toward one another.[48] Affectionate words and
gestures, being attentive and interested ("Tell me more about
that!"), expressing fondness, admiration, and appreciation, humor,
joy, and even surprise ("Wow! That's great!") are all ways couples
can make sure they are meeting their spouse's emotional needs and
demonstrating their love. Since such behavior comes naturally to
neither temperament, both spouses in the melancholic/phlegmatic
marriage will have to make conscious and repeated efforts to in-
grain it as a habit.

Together the melancholic/phlegmatic couple is principled and
dutiful, more comfortable with the modest daily tasks than the
grand or the ostentatious. Both spouses would rather do the right
thing than the showy thing. They find great satisfaction in education and formation, in saving one soul at a time, and in making a
big difference through the little things done well, with love. Low-
key can be just the right key for this faithful, conscientious couple
— especially when they unlock the love that is in their hearts, and
learn to share it boldly with their family, their neighbors, and the
world.

---

[48] John Gottman, Ph.D., *Seven Principles of Happily Married
Couples* (New York: Three Rivers Press, 1999).

Chapter 9

∽

Two Peas in a Pod

"Harmony is pure love,
for love is complete agreement."

Lope de Vega

∞

When both spouses are of the same temperament, they will have double their temperament strengths — and double the drawbacks! These couples, more than others, will bring powerful natural gifts to bear, but they're also more likely to trip over obstacles they are blind to.

The dual-choleric couple will be powerful enough to achieve their ambitious goals, but may neglect each other and bulldoze over their children. The dual-melancholic couple might be idealistic and attentive to detail, but they can forget to express appreciation and emotional warmth to those they love. The dual-phlegmatic couple might be comfortable and unassuming, but might never extend themselves beyond their comfort zone. The dual-sanguine couple might be enthusiastic and generous, but superficial and overcommitted.

Often the kids will point out the weak spots: "Why don't we ever do anything fun?" or "You said you would come to my game!" They may act out or rebel or fail to live up to their potential. This is when we realize the need to go beyond our temperament and grow in virtue — becoming more empathic, more sensitive, more courageous and assertive, and more deeply attentive to our spouse and children.

CHOLERIC/CHOLERIC
An excellent *family*

You might imagine that two cholerics in a marriage would be a recipe for disaster: two leaders, both wanting to take charge, both insisting they're always right. Two generals with no army to command — except, perhaps, their children!

This can certainly happen. The clash may initially be like Katharina and Petruchio's in Shakespeare's *Taming of the Shrew.* However, we know a wonderful double-choleric couple who have been happily married (with many children) for more than twenty years. How do they do it?

Once again, it has to do with understanding, appreciation, and respect. Only in this case, it's not about understanding and appreciating each other's temperamental differences, but their *likenesses* — and then seeking ways to show respect and admiration for each other's particular talents and gifts.

For example, they're both go-getter cholerics, but they have their own clearly delineated sphere of control and area of expertise. Paul admires Rebecca's intelligence and capacity for educating their children at home. Rebecca respects her husband's drive to succeed in his many entrepreneurial ventures. Within their respective spheres, each spouse has free reign, and so long as neither attempts to usurp the other's command, they are content. They can each have the sense of control and accomplishment that cholerics crave, without stepping on each other's toes in the process. True, they sometimes like to offer each other advice, or to make comments or complaints, but the underlying foundation of respect means they seldom allow arguments to escalate harmfully. In fact, cholerics tend to *relish* a good argument. They don't take it personally (most of the time), but instead see the sport in it, or view it as an opportunity to sharpen their skills, or to hash out a proposal and get the best ideas out there on the table. (There's the bottom-line thinking again.)

Teamwork for success

Likewise, competitive cholerics can encourage each other's drive to excel. For example, even though Rebecca just had a baby and homeschools her younger children, she encourages her husband to excel as a high school sports coach. Now, this isn't his "real" job; it's what he loves to do, for his children and their school. But it means that he not only has to work a full forty-hour week (or more) to support his family; he's also gone most nights during the season.

Rebecca doesn't stand in his way. As Paul says, "She wants me to succeed in my work, and I want her to succeed in hers. Neither of us wants to settle for mediocrity." It is significant to note that Rebecca doesn't merely tolerate her husband's long hours spent coaching and working; she actively *encourages* him to put as much effort into them as is necessary to excel. "If you're going to be a coach" she told him, "I want you to be a good one. Why bother spending all that time, and wind up with a losing season?" Rebecca agreed that it would be tough, but she would support him one hundred percent. Every night she would pray with the little ones for the success of their team. And she also made sure to support her husband vocally — especially when he received the inevitable complaints from parents who thought their child wasn't getting enough playing time. Lastly, Rebecca was present at as many games as possible. Their younger children were crawling all over the bleachers, but she was cheering loudly.

As a choleric herself, Rebecca wanted success as much as her husband did; moreover, it simply wasn't in her nature to sit at home complaining that her husband was gone and she was left overwhelmed by the kids. Because they don't whine themselves, cholerics have little patience for whining; this makes other cholerics a good fit for them.

A family of high achievers

It is not surprising that dual-choleric couples also tend to have high-achievement children, successful in academics and sports, and leaders among their peers. You may be tempted to speculate that because Mom and Dad are choleric, their children are genetically programmed for leadership. But not all children of choleric parents will be choleric themselves. Yet even children of other temperaments can be raised to develop some of the focus and goal-orientation that's natural to their choleric parents, especially when those parents have learned not simply to rule their brood by sheer domination and subjugation, as you might find with some less well-formed cholerics.

Cholerics get misty-eyed over the scene in *The Sound of Music* where Captain von Trapp whistles and all seven children fall into formation. That's their kind of parenting! However, it's important for the choleric/choleric couple to moderate their tendency to be over-controlling, and appreciate that having a family (especially a larger one) requires a healthy dose of flexibility. It also helps to have a healthy sense of fun combined with good humor and a realization that these are God's children (not merely *my* children), who therefore will have their own path and mission in life. It is a wise parent (of *any* temperament) who realizes that our task is not to induce our children to do *our* parental will, but to instill in our children an openness to doing God's will.

Cholerics can be mystified by phlegmatic or melancholic kids. There is much the choleric can teach an introverted, cautious child, but angry put-downs, sarcastic comments, and expressions of dis-appointment only push him further into his shell. Cholerics must remind themselves to show respect for their introverted chil-dren's talents — a difficult prospect for the choleric, who can be overly impressed with his own hard-driving way of living — and learn to appreciate the more subtle virtues of patience and mutual understanding.

Ships passing

Even as their path to success lies in taking command of their own spheres of influence, two cholerics will also have to watch out that they don't each become *obsessed* with their own work — commanding officers of two parallel universes. He goes to work every day, discusses politics with his colleagues over a beer after work, battles the traffic, and arrives home late to pay bills and check emails while she puts the kids to bed. She carpools the kids to school, shuttles them to music lessons and sports activities, serves as "snack mom" for the T-ball team, runs the weekly "Kids 4 Jesus" club, collects for a school fundraiser, shops for groceries, ti-dies up the house before her husband gets home, and helps the fourth-grader with his science project and the second grader with spelling. She reads *Good Night Moon* to the toddler. At that point they are both too exhausted to stay up and talk. The next day, it all begins again. Weekends are busy catching up with all the house-hold chores and the kids' sports. Babysitters are hard to find, and they rarely go out as a couple. They seem to be married, but they are functioning in parallel worlds.

This is a common problem for dual-choleric couples. Unless there is a secondary sanguine temperament, the dual-choleric couple can be so driven and ambitious that there is simply no time for fun, relaxation, or even a spiritual life. Personal relationships and social events can be viewed as principally means rather than ends. When this attitude carries over into their marital relationship, it can be harmful. Two busy, driven cholerics will need to set aside time to maintain that emotional and romantic intimacy they originally had at the beginning of their relationship, or else they may find themselves drifting apart, into what is known as the "parallel marriage." These may seem exemplary on the outside, but in reality are quite affectionless.

Cholerics are naturally independent and not emotionally needy. Neither choleric spouse will want to admit to the other that he feels unfulfilled or needs "help." (Of all the temperaments, two cholerics are the least likely to come in for marriage counseling — they're too busy, and they prefer to fix things themselves!) But love requires nurturing, and since the "softer skills" that aid nurturing — showing empathy, expressing your feelings, demonstrating appreciation for other people as ends in themselves — don't come so naturally to cholerics, the dual-choleric couple must make a deliberate and determined effort to build those skills. View it as a challenge!

Cholerics have many natural virtues that enable them to be successful in the world; consequently, they may give short attention to the more subtle, humble qualities of their children or other loved ones. They can be tempted to build their lives on the sand of success, rather than on the true foundation of Christ. The dual-choleric couple will need to be convinced

INSTEAD OF	TRY THIS
"I do all the cooking, cleaning, and taking care of the kids. And I work, too! I do *every-thing* around here!"	"Can you take the kids to their soccer games this weekend, so I can get caught up on some housework?"

that, unless God is first in their life and their marriage, nothing else will be truly successful. Independent, self-sufficient cholerics often find it difficult to accept this truth. But, when they have a relationship with Christ and they have been transformed by grace and the sacrament of Matrimony, the choleric couple that truly places God foremost in their lives will become a formidable force, a dynamic duo for the Lord.

PHLEGMATIC/PHLEGMATIC
Family builders

At first glance, you may think that this is a combination that could never happen. How could either work up the initiative to pursue the future spouse? Would either of them ever get around to proposing?

But somehow, phlegmatics do manage to marry one another. (Perhaps they just hang out comfortably together for so long that they eventually say, "Why not just get married?") And when they do, they make a solid — if not quite scintillating — couple. Their strengths are their stability, their peaceful natures, and their fidelity. They appreciate children and home. Each will respect the other's frugality and sensibility; there will be no outrageous credit-card surprises, no spur-of-the-moment trip to Aruba. Yet they're not likely to become bored with one another (because they are both equally, well, boring). Because they tend to be so family-oriented, so solid and faithful, this combination may be the most commonly occurring and favorable-to-success of the same-temperament unions.

The double phlegmatic couple will tend to be traditional and hardworking. A phlegmatic wife is likely to prefer simple cooking — enjoying baking and preparing unpretentious meals. A phlegmatic husband will appreciate the food, but not require anything fancy. He is content to come home from work to find a hearty meal on the table. They're committed to their children, raising them to be honest and dependable. They volunteer at their church and school, but in steady, unpretentious ways, for they do not seek the limelight.

Bob, an engineer, and Mary, a homemaker and teacher, are just such a phlegmatic couple. Together they provide a humble, yet comfortable home for their seven children. Neither has pretensions or aspirations to greatness; they both proceed one step at a time, keeping their eye on the truly important goal: their relationship with Christ. They find no value or interest in trying to keep up with the Joneses, and they eschew chasing the suburban dream — climbing the corporate ladder, redecorating the house, moving to a more upscale neighborhood. Their warm and simple home provides all they need, without the bells and whistles. That sofa they purchased when they were first married? Why, it is perfectly functional, and why would they want a new one? Those funky black and pink tiles in the bathroom? If they wait long enough, they might come back in style!

Fine and mellow

Because phlegmatics are so easygoing and patient, and have such an accepting and comforting way of dealing with children, it is rare for such parents to incite in their offspring intense rebellion or anger — especially if they've inherited their temperament from Mom and Dad. But even when they have different temperaments, the children of phlegmatic parents tend to go about their business of work and school without causing any sort of major trouble.

That doesn't mean parenting is always a breeze for them. Conflict-avoiding phlegmatic parents may find themselves taken aback or nonplused by an extremely outgoing, demanding, or argumentative child, and mistake some of those different attitudes for rebellion. In such cases, it helps to understand that other temperaments exhibit different typical behaviors, and to be reassured by trusted friends and teachers that their children are behaving within an acceptable norm for kids their age. On the other hand, if the phlegmatic parents don't go out of their way (for it won't come naturally to them) to provide their kids with a strong family structure that encourages effort and excellence, they (especially the phlegmatic ones) might become prone to underachievement.

That last point underscores the major pitfall that awaits dual-phlegmatic marriages: both spouses can be so easygoing that nothing (except the bare minimum needed to survive) gets done! Phlegmatics combine a lack of natural initiative with a high tolerance for putting up with something inferior for a long time, so long as they can still get by. The leaky faucet that would drive a melancholic mad doesn't so much bother a phlegmatic, as long as it doesn't actually keep him awake at night, so he puts off getting it fixed. If the homeowners' association hasn't fined him yet for not taking down those Christmas lights, maybe they could wait until Easter. We know one phlegmatic couple who, instead of de-junking the garage to make more space, just bought a smaller car!

> Phlegmatics do take things personally — they just don't show it.

Our phlegmatic son Ray was commiserating with his phlegmatic girlfriend about the woes of decision-making under pressure (something the easygoing, reluctant-to-offend phlegmatic really does not appreciate).

"I had to decide *on the spot* what to do about dinner!" exclaimed Laura.

"Poor baby," empathized Ray soothingly.

"I don't want to have to make another decision for a week!"

This same tendency applies not only to mundane decisions, but to communication and problem-solving as well. When one spouse is a conflict-averse phlegmatic, family or marital problems often get ignored; swept, as it were, under one side of the rug. With two phlegmatics, problems can get swept under both sides — and stay there! Although remaining faithful and persevering in the marriage commitment, the two phlegmatics can find themselves allowing silent disagreement to lead to withdrawal and a long-term silent treatment.

This is a serious problem to guard against. Recent research suggests that a major cause of divorce is refusal to discuss problems! As Pope Benedict XVI wrote (when he was Cardinal Ratzinger): "One can try to deal with problems either by denying their existence or by facing up to them. The first method is the more comfortable one, but only the second leads anywhere."[49]

"Stretched" to new heights

The low-key phlegmatic couple will benefit from being involved in organizations, projects, and programs that provide a vision and mission to draw them out of themselves and their comfort zone. For example, phlegmatics who are committed to serving the Church will stretch themselves in ways they otherwise wouldn't and will be an example to their children of servant leadership. Both partners in the dual-phlegmatic marriage, naturally prone to extending their aspirations, will benefit greatly from the noble goals and Christ-centeredness that a Catholic marriage offers. When the phlegmatic spouses extend themselves a bit to participate in parish ministries, or together attend marriage retreats or other couples events, they can be inspired to deeper levels of intimacy, too.

Work and family might seem to be sufficient for the dual-phlegmatic couple; however, when they surround themselves with good friends, their world opens up. They are a gift to their friends, who, in turn, bring energy and interest to their lives. Every once in a while it is good for the dutiful, hard-working phlegmatic couple

---

[49]Ratzinger, *Introduction to Christianity*.

to schedule a special getaway or romantic evening, to do something a little wild and spontaneous. After many years of marriage, even though they are as comfortable as an old shoe, injecting some whimsical fun and romance helps keep the fires burning.

MELANCHOLIC/MELANCHOLIC
Perfectionist to the second power

This spousal combination is one of the least common. This may be due to the fact that the melancholics' reserved and cautious nature tends to prevent both parties from taking the initiative necessary to push the relationship along to marriage. Their characteristic pickiness may make it hard for each to overlook the other's faults long enough to fall in love! Or, it could simply be that two introspective types tend not to provide enough "spark" in a relationship to keep the momentum going. Still, although this combination is relatively rare, it isn't impossible. We even know a few: for example, Andrew, a CPA, and his wife, Emily, an art historian, whom we'll meet in a minute.

Mixed blessings

One area in which a melancholic/melancholic couple will have no trouble excelling is delineating boundaries. Because melancholics tend to view things as right or wrong, good or bad, there is little toleration of gray areas. Work does not cross over into family life, children know their place, and the couple will never become overextended in volunteering. The rules are clear, the home is organized, there is a place for everything, and everything's in its place. Although melancholic parents may be tempted to micromanage the details of their children's lives, they tend not to overindulge their offspring. Their children are expected to be responsible, age-appropriately self-sufficient, and respectful. If a child forgets his lunch or notebook, that's a learning opportunity; Mom won't be making a special trip to the school to bring it to him!

Since children usually thrive with structure and well-defined boundaries, this makes for a predictable and smooth-functioning family life. Like two phlegmatics, the melancholic couple tends to provide a safe, secure environment, and to remain focused on career and home.

However, as always, too much of a good thing can become a problem. Melancholic parents can become so focused on structure and rules, on organization and details, that they can become emotionally distant from their children.

If choleric parents can be over-controlling in their desire to teach success, melancholic parents can go too far in their desire to teach self-control. Rather than encouraging their kids to learn the art of decision-making, they want to make the right decisions for them. All this micromanaging and striving for perfection often neglects the bigger picture: the *affective connection* between parent and child that is developed by listening to children, and warmly appreciating them *the way they are*.[50]

Parents who are overly intolerant and judgmental teach their children (who want to please them) not to be virtuous, but to be sneaky. "I told you, no snacks between meals!" admonishes the melancholic parent. The child, afraid of punishment more than desirous of doing right, learns to take cookies when no one's looking. Or, when the eighth-grader is suddenly blossoming into a young teen, melancholic parents might sternly insist that *their* daughter is not going to be boy-crazy! Who will she want to discuss her feelings with — her friends or her parents?

---

[50]The Pontifical Council for the Family writes in *The Truth and Meaning of Human Sexuality* that "parents should learn how to listen carefully to their children . . . to help their children to channel their anxieties and aspirations correctly . . . This does not mean imposing a certain line of behavior, but rather showing the supernatural and human motives that recommend such behavior" (*TMHS*, 50).

Melancholic thrift and cautiousness are also mixed blessings. Two melancholics are likely to stick firmly to the budget, to eschew any crazy purchases, to pay off their credit cards each month, and to have a sensible plan for the future. But they might not be willing to go out to dinner when an intimate evening is called for, or take the family vacation when everyone has a need for relaxation and togetherness. They might also not take the calculated risks that are sometimes needed to get ahead.

Andrew has reached a ceiling in his career — in charge of a small department — but he shies away from reaching higher; he does not wish to risk change, which may require travel and long hours, just to improve his position. Had the opportunity come when he was younger, he might have considered it; however, at this stage in his life, Andrew has all the ts crossed and the is dotted, and he doesn't see the need to shake things up just for a new opportunity. And where a choleric or sanguine wife might actively motivate him to overcome his cautiousness, or a phlegmatic's calm support might give him the confidence to overcome doubts, equally cautious melancholic Emily is happy to watch her husband maintain his professional status quo.

Likewise, Andrew and Emily have lived in the same home for twenty-five years, and although the neighborhood is beginning to show some signs of deterioration, they wouldn't think of moving, because their home has been fully paid for. As they see it, a new mortgage might jeopardize their plans for financially secure retirement. Besides, they worked long and hard to make their home "perfect," remember? One day they *might* cautiously begin to look into the possibility of moving — but certainly not until the market takes an upswing.

A melancholic couple's keen sense of boundaries can also be a double-edged sword. Emily is intelligent, well-educated, and organized, yet she doesn't help her children with their studies; she tells them that they need to learn how to do their own research. In many such areas, she tends to maintain a "respectful distance" when, in fact, her children need a bit more direct involvement. Lacking the counterbalance of a complementary temperament, the dual-melancholic couple will have to watch out that the boundaries they erect do not inadvertently push their loved ones away — or blind them to developing problems.

Emily and Andrew were stunned, for example, when one of their high-achieving children suddenly dropped out of high school, mid-senior year, losing his scholarships. They had missed the warning signs of depression in their talented and driven son, who had been struggling to keep up with his academics and his many extracurricular activities. Children of melancholics often feel an enormous pressure to be "perfect," and sometimes find it too much to bear — a problem that's only amplified when the dual-melancholic parents both have distanced themselves from the scene.

The blues are brewin'!

Dual-melancholic spouses have twice as many opportunities to worry! The melancholic propensity for seeing all the potential pitfalls in a present or future situation is only intensified when *both* are on the lookout for trouble. Problems or worries may take center stage, and soon the couple will begin to feel overwhelmed. When both spouses are feeling overwhelmed by life events — particularly if one or both has a secondary phlegmatic temperament — the couple will be especially vulnerable.

For example, suppose the dual-melancholic couple has just had a new baby and they have begun potty-training the toddler; at the same time, the husband is required to begin traveling for work. The melancholic couple doesn't back down from adding even more stress to an already stressful time: they don't want to lower their expectations, so despite manifest difficulties, they continue with the potty-training! A melancholic couple at Mass will refuse to go in the "cry room" because that would be lowering their standards. Instead, they stress themselves out by trying to keep their five children (aged eight and under) quiet in the front row, constantly shushing them and delivering stern admonitions to stop squirming and pay attention. (The sanguines' kids are, by contrast, crawling under the pews, playing with their Ninja Turtles.) All this only serves to increase the stress level on the parents and their children, and by the end of Mass, Mom is exhausted and Dad is angry.

There is a subtle form of pride that can worm its way into the melancholic marriage; this pride may be hidden behind a facade of humility, but it refuses to back down from the appearance of perfection, despite the huge strain this may place on their interpersonal relationship and their children. In the end, their expectations are not lowered, but their peace and joy is. The stress level rises because both are of the same temperament and there is nobody to offer an "objective" view.

The dual-melancholic couple will have to make a concerted effort to overcome this temptation to be over-controlling, impersonal, and perfectionistic in their relationship with each other and with their children. To do this, first they can utilize the melancholic motivation to live in the truth. It is Christ (not some flaky self-help book) who insists on the priority of charity. And charity is shown through appreciation, affection, forgiveness, and understanding. Secondly, they can appeal to the truth of the five-to-one ratio of appreciation over criticism, to motivate each other to be overt in appreciation and positive expressions.

Finally, when the melancholics realize that over-controlling and perfectionist behavior actually can result in rebellion or a passive-aggressive stance, they will be motivated not to micro-manage as much. Better to achieve this realization sooner than later! Allowing some room for exploration, for new ideas and approaches, and for interpersonal dialogue will ultimately lead to a greater level of cooperation and more mature behavior in their kids, as well as an increase in emotional intimacy between the spouses. Trustful surrender to God's providence does not mean that you surrender your high ideals; only that you surrender the pride that hurts deep intimacy and the emotional connection with your loved ones.

The dual-melancholic marriage is one of intense loyalty. When a melancholic commits to a life-long relationship, there is no turning back. When two commit to each other, you can be sure that, through thick and thin, they will persevere. With attentiveness to positive expressions, their love will blossom. When the melancholic couple has grown in self-knowledge and humility and is committed to their faith, they will find that they can balance their love of noble and holy ideals with delicate charity and magnanimity. Their tendency to worry about the future or to bemoan past mistakes will be offset by a holy confidence and trust in the Lord.

> **INSTEAD OF**
>
> "Who are you, the Queen of Sheba?"
>
> **TRY THIS**
>
> "You look exhausted. Why don't you sit down and I'll bring you a glass of wine?"

SANGUINE/SANGUINE
Co-stars in a prime-time movie!

You might think it easy for two bubbly, fun-loving, and impulsive sanguines to find lasting love with one another. But in fact, this is the rarest combination of them all. One secular research study based on temperament found that out of a pool of five hundred couples, only five — or 1 percent — were dual-sanguine.[51]

Two sanguines may fall head-over-heels in love ... only to change their mercurial minds a few weeks later. When both want to be the center of attention, who will be the audience? While both are out shopping, who will mind the checkbook? We believe that sanguines are more likely to be best friends than lifelong spouses. On the face of it, they're well-suited to enjoying each other's company, but less so to building a long-term conjugal relationship.

Nonetheless, on occasion, two sanguines will marry. And with the grace of the sacrament of marriage, and a deep love for Christ and his Church, they can persevere and find much joy in a deep, abiding relationship.

The sanguine couple will have a fun-loving relationship built on shared interests. Because both are impulsive, outgoing, and adventurous, you might find this pair gallivanting around the globe as intrepid reporters, entertaining students as a teacher couple, or both starting home-based businesses. They enjoy entertaining and are warm, enthusiastic friends and attentive neighbors.

[51]Helen Fisher, Ph.D., "Love Types," *O Magazine* (June 2007). Fisher renames the original four temperaments. She calls the sanguine the "Explorer" and discovers that it is the least likely of all the temperaments to marry the identical temperament.

One sanguine/sanguine couple we know are wonderfully support-ive of each other: there is no argument in this family when Dad wants to spend Sunday watching football with his buddies. Mom just invites her girlfriends over and *voilà!* It's a party! Their kids are pretty happy, too. Their sanguine parents blithely caution them that they won't be able to participate in sports unless they keep up *at least* a "C" average!

Eternal sunshine of the sanguine mind

Sanguines are blessed with good cheer and optimism; however, there is such a thing as *too much* optimism! A dual-sanguine cou-ple can have so much faith in good cheer, happy feelings, pep talks, and the belief that "tomorrow is a new day" that they can avoid the more mundane aspects of married life — like finances, child discipline, or long-term planning. Where cholerics can argue too much, melancholics can be overly critical and pessimistic, and phlegmatics can ignore problems and underachieve, sanguines are liable simply to put on a happy face.

> Research shows that couples who are open to each other's influence have happier marriages.

When both put on a happy face, who will provide the sober realism that is some-times necessary? Not every glass is half-full; not every day is filled with sunshine. Addressing problems head-on and taking a methodical look at possible solutions can be challenges for most of us — but espe-cially for the sanguine couple. Dual-sanguine spouses will first have to acknowledge the hole in their game; often this only occurs when the situation is objectively so dire that they are forced to ac-knowledge the problem: a financial crisis, a child who fails in school, an illness, or a serious marital problem.

Secondly, they will have to listen carefully to what the child, the boss, the doctor, or their spouse is saying. They will need to address the situation and take steps to solve it, ideally instituting some *accountability*. They can promise to hold each other accountable for deadlines, promises, and goals — remembering to measure results, not just good intentions. Because these steps (listening, taking a detailed look at the problem, follow-through) do not come easily to the couple, they may have to bring in a third party: a marriage therapist, a spiritual director, a financial planner, or other professional who will help them address the critical issues and not just skim the surface.

Infinity and beyond!

Another sanguine temptation (especially when there is a secondary choleric temperament) is to become overly involved . . . with everything. The sanguine knows that when he pours his sanguine charisma into a project, people come flocking and marketing soars. Sanguines are often in great demand as promoters — on the job, at school, and in the parish. As a result, they can find themselves drowning or else skimming the surface of everything. Sanguines don't always know when to set a limit on their personal attention and presence. Plus, vanity can compel them to acquiesce!

A dual-sanguine couple's enthusiasm and impulsivity can add up to a lot more commitments than they can actually honor. They make their decisions based on who is asking, or whether it sounds fun, rather than taking a close look at their time, their schedule, or their pocketbooks. So, we have sanguine Dad coaching Little League and volunteering for set construction for the spring musical, and sanguine Mom teaching CCD and bringing meals to the elderly. Oops, they forgot that Dad has to go out of town on business! No problem, Mom can take over Little League practice! The minivan becomes the home-away-from-home, and every night dinners are at Burger King. The grind takes its toll even on the bubbly sanguines, and they begin to get short-tempered with their kids and with each other. By having fingers in too many pies, nothing is accomplished well, and even their important relationships begin to suffer.

A good rule (assuming sanguines will follow a rule) is to think and pray about every decision for twenty-four hours before saying yes. Both sanguines can resolve to speak to their spouse about the request, and to check their calendar (although they may first have to *buy* a calendar). Making reflection *mandatory* is critical for the dual-sanguine couple. They can make a commitment to sit down with each other every evening and review the day. Are we getting overextended as a family? What are the lessons learned from our recent projects? How does this new project fit into our long-term goals? Are we meeting each other's needs? Taking some time out for reflection will not only help them ultimately to accomplish more things well; it will also slow down the frenetic pace (making everything more enjoyable in the long run) and will help them develop interpersonal depth.

Conclusion

∞

Two Become One

Two such as you with such a master speed
Cannot be parted nor be swept away
From one another once you are agreed
That life is only life forevermore
Together wing to wing and oar to oar.

Robert Frost

∞

The human person is made in the image and likeness of God; as fundamentally relational beings, we reflect the Blessed Trinity. God himself, as Pope Benedict wrote, is relatedness, communicability, and fruitfulness.[52]

God said, "It is not good for the man to be alone. I will make a suitable partner for him."[53] Our spouse is our "suitable partner," one whom we have chosen "for better, for worse" and with whom together we seek the door to heaven. And together, we are a sign of Christ's love and mercy in this world.

"[A]nd the two of them become one body."[54] This unity in marriage (a great mystery, as St. Paul puts it to the Ephesians) is more than just a cooperative agreement to get along and raise a family in relative harmony. It is a call to *radical intimacy*: two become one. Yet our Catholic Faith also reminds us that we are born into a sinful, broken world. Sin is not just out there in the world, but is also inside of us, also enters our marriage. So, how can we attain such a unity?

Only God can make this unity possible. It is a gift of the Holy Spirit. We cannot engineer it on our own, nor achieve it merely by developing some techniques. We have to make Christ the foundation of our marriage. Christ himself gives us the strength and grace to live the true meaning of marriage. But this does not mean that we should abandon our own efforts.

[52] Ratzinger, *Introduction to Christianity*.
[53] Gen. 2:18.
[54] Gen. 2:24.

The Temperament God Gave Your Spouse

We hope this book has been helpful to you in your own efforts to create a happy, fruitful, and loving marriage. We hope that your insights into the temperaments, as well as learning some communication skills, will benefit your marriage. When we faithfully practice these techniques (empathy, expressing the positive, using the softened start-up to discuss problems, and avoiding harsh generalizations), we are actually growing in virtue. We will be practicing delicate charity, true humility, and giving up our natural preferences in order to do what is best for our spouse and our family.

When we know ourselves (and our temperament) better, and when we know our spouse better, we will be able to live the sacrament of marriage more vibrantly, and we will have a happier marriage. The *Catechism* tells us that "The harmony of the couple . . . depends in part on the way in which the complementarity, needs and mutual support between the sexes are lived out."[55] We hope that *The Temperament God Gave Your Spouse* has helped you to appreciate (even relish) this complementarity, and that it will provide you with many practical ways to meet your spouse's deepest needs, so that ultimately, your marriage will reach that "master speed" where two become one.

[55]CCC, no. 2333.

Postscript

⁓

When Temperament Is Not Enough

"The glory of God is
the human person fully alive."

St. Irenaeus

∞

The human person is a mysterious unity of body, mind, and spirit. When even one of these aspects is unhealthy, the whole is affected, and the resulting disorders can disrupt both personal and marital unity. Some of these more severe trials include psychological disorders, such as depression, alcoholism and other addictions, and the effects of traumatic events; betrayals of trust, such as pornography use and adultery; and various personality disorders.

Some psychological disorders (such as depression), of course, can lead to serious incapacitation and even death. Yet *all* serious psychological problems can severely impact our intimate relationships and inhibit the mutual understanding and acceptance necessary to marriage. These problems are so serious that simply following the lessons of this book — understanding the temperaments and practicing the communication skills that help build virtue — useful as they are, *isn't enough.*

In fact, problems of this nature can eclipse the impact (positive or negative) of the temperaments, making them even less useful as a marriage-building tool. When we are psychologically wounded, our talents, gifts, and skills can lie dormant — or worse, be warped. Other times, one's natural temperament can be masked by the disorder. For example, a depressed sanguine will not reveal his characteristic sunny optimism, or an alcoholic phlegmatic might exhibit fits of rage.

Our ability to relate to others might also be seriously impaired; for example, a spouse with a personality disorder will tend to react defensively and inappropriately (regardless of his temperament) and will experience great difficulty resolving everyday marital conflicts. Or, someone who is psychologically wounded through a traumatic experience such as sexual abuse may experience difficulty in areas of intimacy.

Our book is not designed to overcome such difficulties. We strongly recommend professional help for anyone who is experiencing them.

Please do not underestimate the need for or value of professional counseling. So often, good Catholics fail to take advantage of all the gifts and opportunities that God is putting in our path, thinking that we should be able to solve all our problems on our own, or that prayer and grace alone will work. Both our own efforts and (of course) God's grace are indeed necessary. Yet God may answer our prayers by putting good doctors, psychologists, psychiatrists, and marriage counselors in our path, and giving us the grace of wisdom to choose them.

You have probably heard the joke about the man who was hanging by his fingertips from a cliff, praying. He turns down the offer of a rope, a helicopter, and a boat, saying, "God will save me!" As he finally falls off the cliff, he asks why God abandoned him. "I didn't abandon you," comes the voice of God. "I sent you a rope, a helicopter, and a boat!"

We Christians believe that the healing power of Christ is greater than any wound. Christ wants us to be fully alive so that we can bring his glory into our lives, our families, and our marriages.

∞

About the Authors

Art Bennett is a marriage therapist and is Director of the Alpha Omega Clinic, a Catholic mental health clinic (www.aoccs.org), and the Manager of Employee Assistance Programs for Triune Health Group (www.TriuneHG.com). He also created a website, www.unityrestored.com, to help those afflicted by pornography. He has more than twenty-five years' experience in consultation and the mental-health field and is a frequent speaker on marriage, workplace, and family issues.

Laraine Bennett has a master's degree in philosophy and is presently a freelance writer with articles published in *Faith & Family*, *The Liguorian*, and *The National Catholic Register*. She writes a monthly column for *4 Marks* and *Catholic Match.com*.

Together, the Bennetts are the authors of *The Temperament God Gave You*, published by Sophia Institute Press. They have lived in California and in Germany and currently reside in Northern Virginia. They have been married for over thirty years and have four children — one of each temperament type!

∞

Sophia Institute Press®

Sophia Institute® is a nonprofit institution that seeks to restore man's knowledge of eternal truth, including man's knowledge of his own nature, his relation to other persons, and his relation to God. Sophia Institute Press® serves this end in numerous ways: it publishes translations of foreign works to make them accessible for the first time to English-speaking readers; it brings out-of-print books back into print; and it publishes important new books that fulfill the ideals of Sophia Institute®. These books afford readers a rich source of the enduring wisdom of mankind.

Sophia Institute Press® makes these high-quality books available to the general public by using advanced technology and by soliciting donations to subsidize its general publishing costs. Your generosity can help Sophia Institute Press® to provide the public with editions of works containing the enduring wisdom of the ages. Please send your tax-deductible contribution to the address below. We welcome your questions, comments, and suggestions.

For your free catalog, call:
Toll-free: 1-800-888-9344

Sophia Institute Press® ◆ Box 5284 ◆ Manchester, NH 03108
www.sophiainstitute.com

Sophia Institute® is a tax-exempt institution as defined by the Internal Revenue Code, Section 501(c)(3). Tax I.D. 22-2548708.